THE TEN GOLDEN RULES
OF LEADERSHIP

THE TEN GOLDEN RULES OF LEADERSHIP

Classical Wisdom for Modern Leaders

M. A. Soupios

Panos Mourdoukoutas

HarperCollins
LEADERSHIP

An Imprint of HarperCollins

The Ten Golden Rules of Leadership

© 2015 M. A. Soupios and Panos Mourdoukoutas

Published by HarperCollins Leadership, an imprint of HarperCollins Focus LLC.

Bulk discounts available. For details visit:
www.harpercollinsleadership.com/bulkquotes
Email: customercare@harpercollins.com

ISBN 978-1-4002-3961-0 (TP)

To all those with **courage, integrity,** and **intelligence**
to know themselves.

CONTENTS

PREFACE

In its many forms, measures, and styles, "leadership" has become a buzzword relevant to almost every facet of modern life. In politics the demands of globalization, sluggish economic growth, explosive sovereign debt, and so on have created public policy challenges that only genuine leaders can resolve. In business, technological advances continue to rapidly redefine every aspect of the corporate world in ways that require new and visionary thinking, the sort of thinking only real leadership can provide. In education, declining student populations, skyrocketing costs, and new instructional methodologies are placing unprecedented demands upon college and university managers that only the most talented will be able to address.

Under these circumstances, it comes as no surprise that a cottage industry has emerged around the subject of leadership. While there are still those who believe that leaders possess innate attributes that cannot be taught, the vast majority believes that leaders can be produced. This second group believes a well-conceived blend of technical skills, real-life work experience, and personal management techniques can result in an effective leader.

While factors such as professional competence and meaningful work experience are undeniably important aspects of any leader's background, there is another variable commonly neglected by those engaged in the leadership debate. It involves a broad view of the human condition, what might be termed a "philosophy of life." It is the premise of this book that the key distinguishing feature of an authentic leader is traceable to a philosophically informed worldview and that the ancient classical tradition is a rich and valuable source of such insights.

The authors advance this position because they see the virtue of philosophical inquiry as a timeless necessity, as valuable for today as it was 2,500 years ago.

THE TEN GOLDEN RULES
OF LEADERSHIP

INTRODUCTION

True Leadership Begins with a Philosophy of Life

There is little doubt that many of the problems afflicting modern society are traceable to an extraordinary dearth of leadership. In politics, business, education, and a myriad of other fields, we are continually reminded of the inadequacies of those in charge. In some cases the deficiencies originate from a lack of technical expertise or experience. There are, for example, occasions when the politics of administrative life allow for the advancement of unqualified individuals; the victory of guile over proficiency is by no means uncommon. In addition, there seems to be a large number of executives who, notwithstanding impressive technical and experiential credentials, are nevertheless incapable of real leadership. Here the problem may lie with a lack of deeper, broader insights, the kind of insights that technical skill alone does not confer—the ability to see the big picture, to connect with members of the organization, to foster a meaningful and productive work environment, and to steer the corporate ship through the challenges of highly competitive markets and new technologies.

This problem forces us to rethink several of the "sacred cows" that have dominated leadership theory in recent years. The first is the notion that virtually anyone can become a leader. Somehow, conventional wisdom has come to assume that the raw material of leadership is latent in just about everyone and that all it takes is a nudge to trigger its unfolding. It is the contention of this volume that views such as these are egregiously misguided and that the special qualities of genuine leadership are remarkably complex and rare. Moreover, we believe that much of the misunderstanding on this point is based on a failure to adequately distinguish mere administration from actual leadership. An effective manager may be able to routinely meet deadlines and proficiently assess budgetary documents, but talents such as these in no way confirm leadership ability. In short, leadership is not the same as management. The former implies a range of insights and talents that are categorically distinct from the mundane execution of daily administrative affairs.

A second sacred cow worthy of being put out to pasture is the idea that leadership can be "manufactured" by following a series of readily identifiable steps. Advocates of this "cookbook" approach to leadership would have us believe that with just a teaspoon of this and a half-cup of that, presto, we create the next captain of industry. Is it any wonder there is a crisis of leadership in this culture? The point is, neither an MBA from Harvard nor years of participating in management seminars can in any way ensure leadership capacity. To put it bluntly, a real leader is not some rabbit waiting to be pulled out of a hat.

How then are we to arrive at legitimate leadership? What are the necessary steps by which men and women might come to govern their work environments with vision and purpose? To begin with, we offer a clear definition of the term "leadership" that differentiates our interpretation from the offhanded views that too often distort the word's meaning. It is the assumption of the authors that leadership is an uncommon composite of skill, experience, and ripened personal perspectives. It is, of course, the last of those elements that sets the real leader apart from those who simply "run" organizations. Ripened personal perspectives are an essential ingredient in a leader's efforts to develop and articulate a sound corporate vision. Real leaders, people like Bill Gates and Steve Jobs, see things more rapidly than does the typical executive. At least in part, their insights are a reflection of an "inner" clarity that allows for fuller concentration on the challenges at hand.

This is why leadership cannot be "done by the numbers," why those who have failed to comprehend the motivating subtleties in their own lives are unlikely to achieve the status of "leader." Simply put, only those men and women who have cultivated a carefully conceived philosophy of life are ready and able to exhibit the kind of workplace mastery suggested by the term "leader." Now for some, invoking the term "philosophy" in this context may seem strangely out of place. To one degree or another, we all have been conditioned to believe that philosophy is at best a kind of noble laziness, a speculative exercise devoid of concrete benefit. Yet it may be that many of the inefficiencies and failures that plague our managerial environments are ultimately related to an inadequate consideration of what philosophy has to offer.

It is for this reason we offer a series of ancient insights presented by some of antiquity's greatest thinkers—men such as Aristotle, Hesiod, Sophocles, Heraclitus, and others. In doing so, we acknowledge the premise set forth in *Republic*, wherein Plato notes that philosophy's lack of usefulness is a myth advanced by those who fail to grasp its larger utility. We agree with Plato's thinking. Accordingly, we maintain that until such time as managers become philosophers or philosophers become managers, we are unlikely to experience any meaningful relief from the debilitating consequences of pseudo-leadership.

- Leadership is not the same as administration.

- The special qualities of leadership are complex and rare. Not everyone can be a leader.

- Leadership cannot be easily manufactured. It is not the result of simple formulas or rules.

- Leadership takes skill, experience, and ripened personal perspectives regarding the nuances and complexities of life.

- Only those men and women who have developed a carefully conceived philosophy of life are capable of genuine leadership.

The reader is advised from the outset that this book is not offered as some kind of "silver bullet" that will magically endow those who consult it with the qualities and virtues of a leader.

Would that the challenges of leadership were so easily obtained! No, the path to authentic leadership is long and steep, and it is not something one can achieve by simply connecting a series of dubiously prescribed dots. Our purpose, therefore, is to elevate and widen perspectives, to foster a spirit of critical self-examination, and to encourage those bold and unconventional attitudes that uniquely distinguish the proven leader.

In the chapters that follow, the philosophy of leadership is codified in ten simple rules:

Rule 1 Know Thyself

Rule 2 Office Shows the Person

Rule 3 Nurture Community in the Workplace

Rule 4 Do Not Waste Energy on Things You Cannot Change

Rule 5 Always Embrace the Truth

Rule 6 Let Competition Reveal Talent

Rule 7 Live Life by a Higher Code

Rule 8 Always Evaluate Information with a Critical Eye

Rule 9 Never Underestimate the Power of Personal Integrity

Rule 10 Character Is Destiny

RULE 1

"Know thyself."
—THALES

Without question, knowledge is an indispensable feature of leadership. Among other things, it is an essential component in addressing the many problems with which leaders are routinely confronted. Accordingly, political leaders claim to have knowledge of how to lead a nation, educational leaders claim to have knowledge that can prepare students for the postgraduate world, and business leaders claim to have the knowledge and know-how to develop products and services that can improve and enrich people's lives (rewarding corporate stakeholders in the process). But, it should be noted that there are two types of knowledge: the factual information that can be acquired by formal education and real-world practices, and knowledge of one's own "inner" world. It is this second category that uniquely establishes the standard of real leadership.

"Know thyself." Understand your inner world, your bright and dark sides, your personal strengths and weaknesses. Self-comprehension is a fundamental precondition necessary for real leadership.

In the sixth century BC Thales, one of the Seven Sages of ancient Greece, reportedly offered the famous instruction "know thyself." This idea of self-inquiry as a mandatory feature of a well-lived life rapidly attained proverbial status among the Greeks. In fact, it was even deemed worthy of inscription on the wall of Apollo's temple at Delphi. Sayings based on great wisdom, such as this one, all have one thing in common, regardless of the time and place in which they occur: they are encouragements to engage in conduct that is demanding and out of the ordinary but nevertheless offers prospects of great reward. Thales' teaching is a classic illustration of this point.

Coming to "know thyself" in a modern sense of the phrase is an immensely difficult task, for several reasons: First, the modern world offers an endless assortment of trivial endeavors that encourage a superficial, nonanalytical existence. Even for those inclined to seek deeper meaning and understanding, the volume of distraction is such that very few are able to engage in anything approximating a meaningful program of self-interrogation.

Second, there are the psychological obstructions we all tend to erect in an attempt to shade our eyes from the glare of troublesome truths. This hindrance to self-understanding is far more formidable than society's many diversionary temptations. Here we are speaking of a powerful tendency to obscure, distort, and fictionalize on behalf of a fabricated reality. Failure to remove these obstacles renders taking stock of oneself impossible. Moreover, those who fail in this regard will never command the intuitions and insights requisite for real leadership. It is essential, therefore, that the would-be leader commit to an agenda of spirited self-indictment, because the most lethal distortions come not from the lips of our opponents or competitors. They tend to flow, instead, from our own hearts.

Third, humans are by nature hedonists—pleasure seekers who instinctively desire ease and comfort over challenge and pain. Here we need to say a few words regarding the issue of truth. The Bible tells us that the truth can set us free. This may indeed be the case in some sense, but it is also the case that truth is not an easy thing to obtain, particularly when it comes to understanding who and what we really are, what we are doing, and why we are doing it. This category of truth, in particular, requires struggle, discipline, and courage. Why? Because here, truth typically involves a good deal of distress and disillusionment. "Knowing thyself" means bringing a fresh transparency to our hidden motives and identities. It involves a process of self-revelation whereby one ruthlessly exposes the frauds and deceits that give us comfort. This is the truth-seeking that sets us free but, as devoted hedonists, we understand it is a path laden with misgiving and it is, therefore, a path rarely traveled.

Fourth, there is the increasingly important obstacle of mass media imagery. With very few exceptions, we are all continually bombarded with portraits of "successful" types who allegedly merit emulation. The ubiquity of these images in television broadcasts, movies, and the Internet has made them an inescapable fact of modern living. The difficulty lies in the fact that these dubious paradigms tend to glamorize lives that are as superficial and inane as they are unreflective. Too readily, we forget that these gilded images are less about truth than they are about selling tickets and boosting Nielsen ratings. As a result, they promote a disreality that suggests there is no particular urgency in considering the larger questions of life, that the struggle to "know thyself" is by and large trivial and unimportant. Instead, we are encouraged to mindlessly embrace popular culture's notion of the good life without any consideration of the meaning and merit of such an existence. Under these circumstances, those who seek higher truth and meaning are assigned the status of eccentric outsider. How does one come to follow the dictum to "know thyself" in a society that powerfully endorses a life lived on automatic pilot—that is, a life lived with little or no commitment to self-examination?

The Four Impediments to Knowing Thyself

1. Everyday distractions that encourage a superficial and nonanalytical existence

2. Psychological obstructions that shade our eyes from the glare of troublesome truths

3. Hedonism, the lack of courage to face and address painful and inconvenient realities

4. The distorted imagery of mass media presentation

Let's be clear about what all this implies for leadership. First, what has just been described explains, in great measure, why there are so few men and women genuinely deserving of the title "leader." The vast majority of people are simply unwilling to explore the dark regions of their inner being. Rather than drop the mask, they keep these areas tightly shuttered in an effort to contain forbidden truths. In so doing, these individuals create a kind of counterfeit reality for themselves, which can place any organization at great risk.

Specifically, this false reality can manifest itself in a variety of distorted policies and approaches. On the one hand, it can produce arrogant and reckless strategies that mirror the executive's ill-reasoned sense of invincibility, like a string of acquisitions to satisfy the ego of the executive suite rather than to advance the cause of the organization. In other words, the program cannot possibly fail because "I" conceived and developed the program! A confident leader can be a valuable asset for an organization. However, when self-assurance crosses the line and become rash presumption, the executive turns from an asset to a liability.

Another form of sham reality attributable to leaders who resist self-examination is the idea of "entitled" success. "I was a successful hedge fund manager on Wall Street; I can turn this retailer around" or "I was successful in refurbishing an electronics gadget retailer; I can do the same for a department store chain." Here again, there is a powerfully distortive understanding of who the executive is and what he or she can reasonably expect in terms of outcomes. Apparently, there are some administrators who entirely discount the possibility of failure simply because they believe they are entitled to succeed. This logic can have a devastating effect upon the organization to the extent that hubris tends to foster complacency, which in turn radically heightens the prospect of failure. In fact, corporate history is littered with stories of great corporations that declined and eventually disappeared because arrogant leaders took success for granted, including Eastman Kodak, Lehman Brothers, Enron, and Global Crossing.

Real leaders understand that success is never something that can be claimed as a birthright. It requires continuous effort as well as a certain humility that acknowledges the possibility of defeat. These insights are understood best by those who have candidly cast a critical light in their own direction. Simply put, leaders who fail to understand their own deficiencies and limitations become performers in mock dramas in which the actors no longer understand that they are acting. The organization then is made to pay the price.

Knowing oneself means the end of role-playing. It involves casting a harsh and unforgiving light upon a variety of self-exonerating falsehoods. Needless to say, attaining an unvarnished view of oneself is an intimidating process. It takes a good deal of nerve to unmask those reassuring lies we so enjoy telling ourselves. But, then again, it also takes a good deal of nerve to be a real leader.

To follow the dictum to "know thyself," would-be leaders must:

- Explore the dark side of their inner being, the frauds and deceits that nurture a counterfeit reality

- Reveal psychological deficiencies and troublesome truths

- Cast a harsh and unforgiving light at self-exonerating falsehoods

- Commit to an agenda of spirited self-indictment— an honest self-discovery process designed to dispel self-induced frauds

In conclusion, self-comprehension is a fundamental precondition of an effectively lived life. In addition, we believe this principle has particular relevance for any man or woman intent on assuming the reins of leadership. As for those who shrink from the task of confronting their own weaknesses and shortcomings, it is highly unlikely they will attain anything approximating the extraordinary status suggested here by the term "leader." How can those who remain blind to themselves lead others?

THE GOLDEN LEADERSHIP GRID

- Explore your inner being.

- Understand who you are. Be ready to commit to an agenda that uncovers and dispels psychological deficiencies, personal insecurities, and self-deceptions.

- Develop an accurate and unambiguous self-understanding that nourishes, informs, and updates everything you do.

- Be quietly confident without being vain or proud.

RULE 2

"Office shows the person."
—PITTACUS

O f all the many problems facing today's business world none is more critical than the quality of the work environment. In the absence of an affable work setting, employee loyalties quickly dissolve. According to U.S. Department of Labor statistics, employees typically remain in their position for only about two years. Surveys designed to explain this remarkable mobility suggest that the number one reason for employee exit is a disagreeable workplace. The implications of this rapid turnover are clear: The organization forfeits the time, energy, and resources it invested in recruitment and suffers the effects of having employees who lack meaningful commitment to the organization. How can organizations motivate staff members who are constantly seeking vocational alternatives?

Negative work settings do not occur spontaneously. Almost without exception, this potentially lethal failure can be traced to managerial deficiency and more often than not, to the abusive misapplication of power on the part of the manager. Nothing will more rapidly disenchant and alienate workers than a manager who delights in resorting to the stick as opposed to the carrot.

Office Shows the Person

The assumption of authority brings out the leader's inner world. It reveals whether the leader has undergone a process of honest self-discovery that allows for the productive application of power.

One of Thales' colleagues on the list of Seven Sages was the ruler of Mytilene, a man named Pittacus (circa 600 BC). After governing his city for a decade, Pittacus voluntarily relinquished his power and retired. The ancient author Diogenes Laertius recorded a number of famous sayings traditionally attributed to Pittacus, the most famous being "office shows the man." Above all else, this maxim addresses the critical issue of power and its effects. Implicitly it contains two premises. First, that the investment of power—in other words, granting a leader meaningful authority—is the trigger that will rapidly reveal that person's inner qualities. Second, that power not only has a potential to disclose who a person really is; it also has the capacity to corrupt. We need to examine both of these ideas.

Anyone who has been involved in hiring a new employee understands that the resume, the reference letters, the interviews, and so on provide at best only an opaque view of a candidate's actual identity. Throughout the various phases of the hiring process, the real person is easily concealed by a series of highly stylized rituals and procedures. In terms of getting at the core personality, the procedure remains as superficial as it is cosmetic, with the result that one never really knows the person behind the mask until the employee is "up and running."

These points are particularly noteworthy in the case of senior personnel, the people who are assigned important leadership roles in an organization. For these individuals, the investment of power has an all-important diagnostic potential. Power will invariably reflect what no resume ever does, namely the psychological and spiritual disposition of the person. And here, of course, we are brought back to the points made in the discussion of Rule 1. What is soon to be revealed in the newly hired "leader" is whether or not a process of honest self-discovery has taken place. If the battle to dispel self-induced fraud has been successfully waged, if indeed the individual has heeded Thales' "know thyself," that achievement will be mirrored by the manner in which power is utilized.

Those who enjoy a philosophically informed understanding of life will use their authority in an enlightened fashion to advance the organization's legitimate purposes. In such hands power becomes an instrument of integrity and conscience capable of yielding immeasurable benefit to the workplace. But what of those who have failed to look inward along the lines described here? What of those who do not know themselves but who nevertheless enjoy the prerogatives of power? What will office reveal about these men and women?

Leaders Must Understand the Limitations of Traditional Recruitment Mechanisms

- Conventional recruiting processes can identify and test the technical and managerial skills of prospective leaders.

- However, they cannot unveil the inner world, the psychological and spiritual disposition of the person. In particular, these processes cannot reveal the all too common tendency to abuse power.

These are the circumstances that compel a consideration of power's corruptive tendencies and the many destructive effects such corruption routinely bring. Lord Acton, a nineteenth-century British historian, is famous for having noted that "power tends to corrupt and absolute power corrupts absolutely." Pittacus, and the ancient Greeks in general, fully understood the logic of Acton's observation. They recognized that the prospect of exercising power, and particularly the ability to apply power in an ego-driven manner, holds an irresistible charm for many people.

Making sense of how all this works is impossible without considering the mental state of those inclined to abuse authority. In the majority of cases, the misuse of power is undoubtedly a direct result of psychological deficiency. Under these circumstances power becomes a kind of compensatory asset. It is employed as a defense mechanism to offset feelings of inadequacy and vulnerability. In other words, the abusive application of power is the only way some leaders can attain a sense of security and confidence in life. They have a need to control and dominate everything and everyone around them. Under these circumstances organizational purposes take a backseat to the psychological needs of the manager. If a situation such as this goes unremedied, it can reduce the work environment to little more than a dysfunctional psychodrama in which unit morale and worker productivity are severely compromised.

Needless to say, work settings that are healthy and productive are not the result of spontaneous good fortune. Establishing and maintaining such an environment requires a complex range of assets and activities that have little to do with chance. But of all the many ingredients required for success, the most important by far is quality leadership. In good times, the leader maximizes institutional momentum and formulates plans to sustain growth and market advantage, sharing the rewards of success with all members of the organization. In bad times, the leader has the courage and insight to develop new strategies while simultaneously maintaining high levels of worker morale and commitment by spreading the cost of painful adjustments among all organization stakeholders, beginning with headquarters.

In short, the role of a good leader is critical under all conditions, and it is for this reason too that failures of leadership will virtually ruin the organization. And of all the many potential shortcomings an assumed leader might bring to an organization, none is more lethal than arbitrary applications of power. Supervisors who constantly micromanage, who second-guess every subordinate decision, who gleefully await any and all opportunities to criticize and bully, are a toxic presence in any environment. Their abuses will predictably waste corporate resources, destroy worker motivation, compromise institutional loyalties, and create debilitating resentments more rapidly than any other managerial failing—prompting the most talented employees to jump ship.

It goes without saying that correcting the misconduct of a bully manager is no easy task. As we have suggested, much of the underlying explanation for this form of behavior is deeply rooted in the psychological makeup of the individual. It is unlikely, therefore, that an occasional rebuke is likely to alter such conduct. Under these circumstances the organization has two options.

First is the shock therapy approach, wherein bedside manner is put aside in favor of blunt and unambiguous reprimand. One way of accomplishing this is to solicit anonymous written assessments of the supervisor's activities from the victims. Subordinates might be asked to respond to a set of questions such as the following: Is the supervisor's conduct fair and objective? Does the supervisor encourage an honest and open exchange of ideas? Does the supervisor interact with subordinates in a constructive and professional manner? Of course, the organization must guarantee that this process will operate on a reprisal-free basis; that is, no punitive action will be allowed against the unit or any individual member of the unit. The findings should then be presented to the supervisor in no uncertain terms. If the data indicates a consistent pattern of abuse, the organization must use this information to put the administrator on formal notice that such conduct is unacceptable. The supervisor might then be required to attend training sessions specializing in the effective application of authority, and should be notified that a second survey will be conducted in a few months' time.

If the second round of data indicates little or no change in the administrator's despotic conduct, the organization should not hesitate to exercise option two: relieve that person of his or her responsibilities. Given the potential negative consequences of allowing such an individual to continue, there is no real option in such a case. Moreover, periodic bloodlettings along these lines will convey a poignant message to others inclined to abuse power and, even more important, they will signal the institution's genuine concern with issues of corporate "justice." The significance of this last point cannot be overstated to the extent that it can restore worker confidence in the organization and lessen the likelihood of worthy employees seeking less-authoritarian pastures.

Authority becomes an instrument of integrity and conscience, nurturing a healthy and productive workplace environment.

True leaders who have developed a philosophy of life and use authority to advance the causes of the organization.

True leaders display moderation and courage in navigating the organization in both good and bad times.

Office can reveal two kinds of leaders:

Pseudo-leaders who have failed to develop a philosophical understanding of life misuse authority.

Power is deployed as a defense mechanism to offset feelings of inadequacy, creating an unhealthy work environment.

Genuine leaders have no need for or interest in browbeating staff members; they understand that administrative styles relying upon fear and coercion are ultimately counterproductive. Abusive leaders serve neither the interests of the organization nor the career objectives of the leader. Rather than conduct themselves in a dictatorial manner, real leaders offer object lessons in the fair and enlightened application of authority. Simply put, they lead by dignified example, turning subordinates into "believers" who will go that extra mile to advance institutional objectives. Above all, they recognize that true leadership does not come from the crack of a whip. In fact, reliance upon such methods is often proof of administrative failure. No, authentic leaders embody a special wisdom that appreciates how often the cooing of a dove is more profound and productive than the roar of a lion.

In conclusion, office and the use of authority usually reveal something about leaders that standard recruitment processes don't. Specifically, power discloses whether or not a person has disposed of the psychological deficiencies that negate the possibility of real leadership. Unfortunately, revelations such as these tend to come after the fact: after the organization has extended a job offer. Accordingly, the institution should be prepared to move swiftly against any leader who clearly cannot be trusted to exercise authority in a constructive manner.

THE GOLDEN LEADERSHIP GRID

- The assumption of power uncovers the spiritual traits of the person.

- Office reveals two types of leaders:

  - True leaders use power wisely, lead by example, create a pleasant work environment, and advance the cause of the organization.

  - Pseudo-leaders bring to the office the ills of their inner world, use power as a compensatory asset, and create a hostile work environment.

- Institutions must have a proper mechanism in place to rid themselves of pseudo-leaders sooner rather than later.

RULE 3

"Nurture community in the workplace."
—PLATO

W ell-functioning corporate communities and positive group sentiment are the foundation of the modern workplace. They gather and focus the energies and resources of business organizations in the pursuit of institutional goals. Yet the skills involved in creating these communities are rarely stressed in business schools or textbooks. These cooperative units do not arise spontaneously. They tend to be uniquely related to the talents of the leader.

Community development and positive group sentiment are virtues leaders must nurture by providing the right support, guidance, and incentives.

Perhaps the most noted of Plato's many dialogues is a work titled *Republic*, in which the philosopher outlines his theory of the ideal state. Among the many premises contained in this famous text is an extended argument on the necessity of social unity. There is little doubt that Plato was reacting against the divisive activities of certain powerful clans that routinely advanced their own cause at the expense of the larger welfare. In response, he insists that there is no greater evil than discord and faction and no greater good than the bonds of communal sentiment.

In analogizing these principles, Plato referred to an injured finger. At the moment the finger suffers its distress, it is not the finger alone that experiences the pain. Rather, the entire body participates in a kind of sympathetic reaction to the discomfort. This is how a healthy body functions, and also how a healthy society operates. Only when a social unit enjoys a harmony of value and loyalty will it be able to attain its desired objectives. In great measure, this explains why Plato makes the establishment and preservation of the common good the primary task of the philosopher-king.

Despite the passage of 2,400 years, many of the points offered by Plato remain remarkably meaningful for today. When, for instance, he insists that the good of a few must not be allowed to prevail over the commonweal; when he argues that disunity and faction are disruptive forces that jeopardize the efficient functioning of society; and when he identifies friendship and community as essential ingredients in a well-ordered state, Plato advances a social doctrine whose worth and validity are timeless. Moreover, Plato's reasoning has a particular significance for modern executives who, as we have suggested, need to become something more than mere administrators and devote themselves instead to becoming the corporate equivalent of philosopher-kings (or -queens).

Admittedly a suggestion such as this may seem exceedingly naive to some, but in truth the potential benefits to an organization are undeniable. Indeed, some of the world's most successful companies have attained their status because they enjoy a philosophy of leadership that reflects the virtue of "team," in this case the creation of various communities within the larger institution. They understand both the logic and the efficacy of an environment in which the workforce is skillfully forged into productive units that approach the term "we" as an essential part of the corporate culture. Needless to say, achieving this cooperative "sweet spot" is often a challenging task for two reasons. First, there is often a pronounced unwillingness on the part of some employees to genuinely embrace group integration. Accordingly, "team" status can neither be assumed nor taken for granted. Second, the creation of corporate communities requires special skills on the part of the team leader. All too often, these abilities are not part of the administrator's standard skill set to the extent that they require keen psychological insight vis-à-vis subordinates and, more important, a critical willingness to self-assess.

The two obstacles to creating corporate communities:

1. Individualism—"I" before "We"
2. Lack of willingness to critically self-assess

With regard to team formation, it is important to note how difficult the process can be to establish. It is also important to understand the root causes for this complexity. In addition to obstacles stemming from the particular biographical history of an individual staff member, there are also powerful cultural forces working against the ready formation of teams. American culture has an almost romantic fascination with the virtues of the individual. We tend to heap praise upon few figures in society with more zeal than the man or woman who triumphs over adversity by the persistent application of personal assets. For most Americans, there is something irresistibly compelling about the rugged, lonely individual who against all odds audaciously marches to victory driven by little more than sheer willpower.

Despite our strong affection for Horatio Alger stories, the truth remains that very few people ever approximate the imagery we find so enticing. True, there may be a handful of individuals who rise to the top based on some unique talent, but the vast majority of those who "make it" in America are men and women who avail themselves of preexisting social networks. In other words, behind the portrait of the self-made individual is the reality of a complex system of collective support mechanisms—institutions, organizations, groups, and so on, many of which play a major role in both the cultivation of the individual's talents as well as the individual's ascent.

Unfortunately, the reality of all this is too often lost amid the myth of the maverick genius, with the result that many individuals view group participation as a kind of submersion that threatens the expression of their special abilities. Therefore they are often disinclined to invest themselves in such processes, even when the organization mandates involvement. However, rejecting these larger social attachments may lead to cutting oneself off from a critically important collective resource that could help achieve important gains for both the company and the team member. One of the most essential activities of a genuine leader is to clearly articulate these points to subordinates, to help them understand that the logic of collective action is beneficial to organization and individual alike.

Specifically, those who resist integration must be made to see that the team benefits from their inclusion just as they benefit from being part of the team. A well-ordered group such as this functions as a force multiplier in which the potency of both the unit and the individual enjoy mutual enhancement. Accordingly, when an institution is faced with some serious challenge or finds it necessary to develop a succession of new and innovative strategies, there is no finer instrument than a well-functioning team.

What the leader should do:

- Defy the myth of maverick genius.
- Help subordinates understand the benefits of cooperation.

How is the phrase "well-functioning" being used here? The key defining elements include the following: a strong sense of loyalty and commitment to the organization, a spirit of genuine camaraderie among team members, and a consistent willingness to subordinate personal interest in favor of the larger good. With these assets in place, an organization is much more likely to enjoy the many advantages of an enhanced decision-making process.

By way of illustration, let's imagine a team meeting in which eight colleagues gather to formulate plans for an important new product line. Though there are obvious pressures, the atmosphere at the meeting remains open, tolerant, convivial. As the meeting unfolds, a flurry of innovative ideas are put forward. There is no sense of constraint or restriction. Everyone feels perfectly at ease in presenting a wide variety of novel and provocative suggestions. The subsequent discussions are candid, even blunt, but they never deteriorate to a level of ill-spirited bickering.

In the energetic give-and-take that follows, most of the proposals are ultimately rejected but a few ideas survive the group's critical scrutiny and appear to have real merit. Eventually, a consensus emerges that all members of the group freely endorse. Everyone at the table feels a strong sense of personal investment in the final proposal. In addition, participants leave the session confirmed in their belief that the process itself had integrity—in other words, no administrative contrivance and no prearranged agendas.

The Key Elements of a Well-Functioning Team

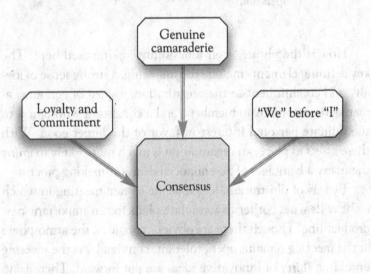

What has just been described is a snapshot of a well-oiled problem-solving machine, the likes of which every organization must strive to create. The beauty of such an instrument lies in its potential to tap into the creative energies of individual team members while simultaneously benefiting from refinements afforded by a collective assessment process. Now the question is, how does one go about creating and directing such a team? Without hesitation, we suggest that the responsibility and the challenge lie primarily with the leader. In addition, we believe that this aspect of leadership responsibility is one of the most demanding tasks a manager will be called upon to perform. To begin with, team composition is critical. The leader must carefully assess various personalities with an eye toward the group dynamic likely to result. Is this candidate too passive and therefore unlikely to honestly argue from conviction? Is this individual too aggressive and likely to intimidate and demoralize other members of the group? Is this person a follower who merely goes along with whatever appears to be the prevailing sentiment? In matters such as these "chemistry" is all important, and it therefore falls to the leader to assemble a proper mix of members capable of honest, cooperative, and productive thinking.

Another important feature of the team process concerns the supervisory function of the leader. Here it is imperative that the leader understand the need for a subtle balance. Too often, leaders tend to define their role in environments such as these as purely facilitative. This can become a most costly mistake. While there is no question the leader must support and advance the collective enterprise, there is also no question that facilitation must never be confused with abdication. In the absence of the leader's continuous guidance, a variety of serious missteps can occur, any one of which may easily compromise the process. For example, without the leader's judicious application of authority, the group can disintegrate into three or four antagonistic camps, a phenomenon known as subgroup formation. This deteriorative potential can result in a total collapse of the team dynamic.

Another situation that demands the leader does in fact lead is the tendency for what might be termed "thematic drift." Group brainstorming can result in a wide and interesting range of new ideas, but these sessions can also produce a great deal of extraneous thinking that has little or no relevance for the organization. The effective team manager always seeks to keep the group grounded, focused, and on point.

A final illustration of why it is imperative that a leader remain actively engaged in directing team activities involves the continuous potential for personnel mismatch. Let's imagine that even after a rigorous screening process an individual is placed on the team but then rapidly displays a variety of negative tendencies that seriously impair the process. Though provided every opportunity to fully affiliate with colleagues, this individual instead chooses to function as a kind of freelance figure who remains detached and uncommitted to almost all group activities and purposes. Under these conditions the leader must exercise executive authority and remove the impediment. No hesitation should be shown in taking such action.

All of this suggests the leader must assume a balanced approach in directing the affairs of the team. On occasion, the leader can afford to employ a rather laid-back management style. However, when circumstances warrant, the leader must be prepared to govern team activities in a direct and definitive manner. This is particularly important as a means of averting one of the chief contaminants of viable team process: groupthink. The leader must ensure that the process is not commandeered by some prevailing mindset that discourages candor and creativity. Conceptual incest along these lines has the potential of negating every benefit that team activity might bestow. Accordingly, the unit must function as a safe haven where offbeat and heterodox thinking is esteemed and encouraged.

It remains to consider to what degree the team leader should become an integral part of the collective process. As already suggested, under no circumstances must the leader relinquish authority on behalf of some "cheerful" unity. A team is not a social club. It is an institutional subunit dedicated to yielding concrete advantage to the organization. At the same time, however, the leader must recognize that a high-handed application of authority will have lethal effects upon the group's ability to function. In other words, real leaders resist the temptation to reduce the team to a personal ego platform whose ultimate aim is to advance the name, image, and reputation of the leader. Motives such as these are impossible to hide from the group, and they inevitably result in a debilitating cynicism that will negate every potential benefit the group process has to offer. The lesson here is as simple as it is obvious: Whenever possible and fitting, the team leader opts for "we" as opposed to "I."

Finally, the leader must take special care not to monopolize those celebratory occasions when the organization acknowledges

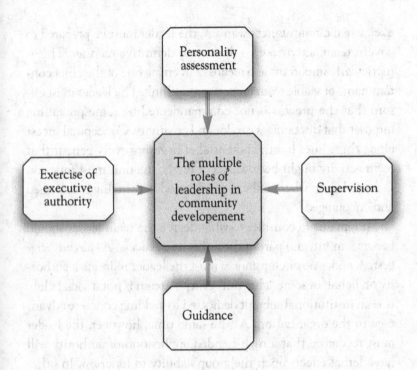

achievement. If, for example, a team succeeds in developing some new strategy that results in substantial advantages to the institution, the team leader must not demand center stage or seek a disproportionate share of the accolades.

Credit for all successes, great and small, must be shared on an equitable basis. Real leaders will be secure enough and intelligent enough to appreciate the wisdom of a magnanimous gesture on such occasions. Not only will this sharing of praise earn the leader the respect and appreciation of group members, it will also set the stage for future team successes by safeguarding the group's cohesive qualities. It is fully appropriate, therefore, that corporate commendations be extended to all who contributed to the group's achievement.

Leaders:

- Shouldn't monopolize celebrations of corporate achievement

- Should assign the appropriate credit to community members who contributed to corporate success

- Must appreciate the wisdom of magnanimous gestures in corporate celebrations

We began this chapter with an assertion by Plato that there is no greater good than a strong sense of community. In offering this opinion, the philosopher was referring to society as a whole, but his logic is undoubtedly meaningful for any organization, be it private or public sector. Almost all of the available evidence suggests that institutions in which "team" is a prioritized aspect of corporate culture possess substantial advantages over the competition. The reasons are not difficult to understand. Any organization that enjoys a genuine spirit of fellowship among its employees as well as strong institutional loyalties cannot fail to achieve its fair share of victories. And, of course, it goes without saying these strategic assets are all directly related to the enlightened administration of the manager turned philosopher (leader).

THE GOLDEN LEADERSHIP GRID

Leaders must:

- Recognize the importance of corporate communities and well-functioning teams for the modern workplace

- Foster a culture of cooperation and collaboration by defying the myth of the exceptional individual, and by explaining the corporate gains of working together

- Perform personality assessments of potential team members

- Guide and supervise teams

- Apply executive authority as needed

- Refrain from monopolizing success, rather recognizing and distributing acknowledgments across the community

RULE **4**

"Do not waste energy on things you cannot change."
—ARISTOPHANES

The word "change" has become a critically important term in today's corporate world for two reasons. First, the spread of globalization with its rapid development of integrated markets has made change a constant and unavoidable aspect of doing business. Second, the rapid advancement of IT technologies has produced an environment in which business models are in a continuous state of flux.

If corporations are to survive and prosper in such change-driven environments, "they should strike out on new paths rather than travel the worn paths of accepted success," to use John D. Rockefeller's words. But steering clear of old paths and strategies is often a difficult thing to achieve. Old habits and institutional inertia are powerful forces that distort the need for change and innovation. In addition, they can link the institution to policies and programs that have little or no prospect of success while wasting vast amounts of valuable resources.

There are many illustrations of ways in which conventional wisdom can obscure sound business practices. For example, consider the idea that subcontracting and outsourcing can help a company become more efficient and effective. While these policies helped PC makers cope with intensified competition brought about by globalization, they failed to protect the industry against another, more brutal form of competition—alternative products such as tablets and smartphones. Similarly, the trusted maxim that concern for core business is the key to competitive advantage can no longer be seen as a guarantee of profitability. The failure of East-man Kodak and the gradual decline of Xerox prove that not all such strategies work in a rapidly changing business environment. As a result, leaders must assume a posture of flexible response: quick to take advantage of new opportunities, and quick to discard practices that offer little prospect of benefit.

Do not waste resources and energies on things you cannot control and things you cannot change.

In the spring of 421 BC, at the annual festival dedicated to the god Dionysus, the Athenian playwright Aristophanes presented a comedy titled *Peace*. At one point in the performance one of the characters is heard to say "never will you make the crab to walk straight." The message is clear: There are some events and circumstances that are unlikely to change, no matter how aggressively we attempt to alter them. This observation was offered in the famous burlesque style that made Aristophanes the master of Old Comedy. Nevertheless, there is a serious insight contained here that has little to do with comedic revelry. It involves the important skill of knowing when to suspend efforts to control or transform situations that ultimately defy modification.

On the surface, this may all seem quite obvious and in little need of detailed clarification. However, the situation is actually much more complex than it appears initially, given the psychological disposition of many leaders. The men and woman who rise to the top of most organizations are not the sort of people who are inclined to walk away from challenges. They tend to be hard-charging types who relish the exhilaration of long odds. Specifically, they seek opportunities to succeed where others have failed, and toward this end they are routinely prepared to redouble their own efforts and those of their subordinates on behalf of achieving some unprecedented goal.

Needless to say, there is much to be admired in a leader who exudes the confidence, energy, and commitment to tackle almost any assignment, even when the odds are stacked against the endeavor. This kind of "can do" attitude is obviously an invaluable leadership asset that no organization can afford to be without. There are, however, limits and liabilities associated with the aggressive executive who refuses to take "no" for an answer. In the real world, no leader ever manages to resolve every problem and accomplish every task, no matter how talented that person may be. Inevitably there will be times when too many variables lie beyond the control of the executive, with the effect that no application of effort and ability can secure a positive outcome. But is the leader one who is willing to accept the reality of such a situation, or among those who continue to insist that they can compel the crab to walk straight?

- Leaders must have the wisdom to distinguish between things that are in their control and things that aren't.

- Things leaders can control are corporate goals and priorities, the selection of people to staff key positions, the choice of corporate partners and

(continued)

associates, and the location of different corporate units and divisions.

- The things that are not under the leaders' control include government policies and the activities of competitors.

- Real leaders must allocate their resources and energies to the things they control and steer away from the things that are beyond their control.

It is the contention of the authors that genuine leaders possess a wide variety of valuable discernments regarding both the organization and themselves. Not the least of these insights is a clear and candid recognition of their own limitations. Real leaders understand and readily accept the practical constraints that inevitably delimit executive achievement. In particular, they are not guided by some messianic self-concept regarding their own capacities. In other words, effective leaders do not conceive of themselves as wonder workers destined to succeed in every venture and policy. Rather, they are objectively realistic about the challenges and uncertainties that complicate every work setting and, more to the point, they fully grasp the consequences of failing to disengage from projects and policies that offer little prospect of favorable outcome.

By way of illustration, consider the following example. Let's imagine that a highly accomplished executive has assumed responsibility for an important but extremely challenging venture. Significant amounts of institutional resources, both budgetary and human, are reallocated to the undertaking. The managing executive tackles the activity with the same full-throttle enthusiasm that earned the person a sterling reputation throughout the organization. A year into the project, however, few if any gains have been realized. In great measure, the lack of tangible success was traceable to a series of new regulatory requirements imposed by the government. All efforts to secure exemption, as well as those aimed at temporary postponement, proved fruitless. In addition, the costs associated with redirecting the program in a manner that might lessen government control proved to be prohibitively expensive. To make matters worse, "team" chemistry deteriorated dramatically as the project's many shortcomings became more and more apparent. Initially, the group's esprit de corps was a cause for confident optimism but as the obstacles to success mounted, a debilitating divisiveness took hold. Increasingly, accusation and recrimination became the prevailing group dynamic. Despite continuous attempts to restore collective unity, the leader was unable to reverse the team's downward spiral.

Any neutral observer assigned the task of assessing this situation would quickly come to the following conclusion: The organization must redirect its resources and energies in more productive directions. But none of this may seem so obvious to a leader not used to admitting failure—real or perceived! The point is, of course, that real leaders are disinclined to squander time and effort on projects unlikely to yield solid returns. They are quick to assess a losing proposition, learn from the situation, and move on to more profitable activities. Of course swallowing one's pride in such matters is never an easy thing, with the result that many executives find it necessary to explain away ineffectiveness by elaborate excuse-making, all aimed at self-exoneration. Efforts such as

these are counterproductive on several levels. First, they are unlikely to convince anyone familiar with the situation that the team
leader shares no responsibility for the project's unimpressive results. Second, any attempt along these lines sends a highly negative signal throughout the organization regarding the leader's
candor and personal sense of security. Nothing will compromise
the corporate image of a manager more rapidly than an unwillingness to forthrightly assume responsibility for failure. Honest failure
on the part of a leader can be forgiven, but the hypocritical refusal
to "man-up" is a sin whose memory is almost impossible to erase.

Of course, being honest about failure is easier said than done.
Especially when it comes to leaders of publicly traded companies
who are subjected to the discipline of Wall Street and the close
scrutiny of the media, quarter after quarter. How can leaders tell
stockholders—their actual bosses—they have failed to enhance
the value of the corporation they were entrusted to lead? How can
they stand by seeing the company stock halved, just because they
missed analyst earnings or revenue estimates last quarter or because
they gave inaccurate guidance for the next quarter? How can they
stand the criticism of the financial press, which may label such a
leader the worst CEO of the year? Moreover, how can they deal
with activist investors and corporate raiders who are eager to
change leadership?

Simply put, the shortsightedness of Wall Street and the media
has created a culture of "loss aversion" among the leaders of publicly traded corporations that creates a bias against change—better
to stay with the old secure business than venture into new products
risking big losses. This explains why the founders of some successful private companies decide not to take them public and why the

founders of some publicly traded corporations decide to take them private (examples are Dell, H.J. Heinz, and Levi Strauss & Co.), and why some publicly traded companies have stopped giving quarterly guidance so they can concentrate on the long term (for example, Unilever).

Real leaders:

- Learn how to disregard failing projects that can damage the organization

- Share responsibility for whatever failures occur

- Study and learn from the failures

- Redirect resources and energies to more promising projects

All who would hope to attain the status of genuine leader are well advised to consider the counsel presented by Aristophanes. Any managers lacking the essential skill of knowing when to avoid some endeavor or when to disengage from a project devoid of prospect are a detriment to the organization as well as to themselves. It is important to be clear about what the term "skill" implies in this context. It is certainly not a reference to techniques acquired from a book or from some training seminar. Rather, the ability in question is ultimately a reflection of the ego state and character of the leader. Simply put, real leaders have the confidence and courage to acknowledge their own limitations. They are secure enough in their own being to accept the reality that on occasion, even they are incapable of dispensing miracles. In addition, these men and women are prepared to formally acknowledge their role in enterprises that fail to bear fruit. They understand, as difficult as it might be, that an honest mea culpa is an essential leadership trait that speaks volumes to a manager's maturity and merit. Indeed, one might even argue that periodic confessions along these lines are one of the most powerful means by which a leader can secure the respect and loyalty of subordinates. In sum, it is a fool's errand to seek to alter the lateral stride of a crab, and even more foolish to deny the wastefulness in attempting to do so.

THE GOLDEN LEADERSHIP GRID

Leaders must:

- Have the wisdom to define and distinguish between the things that are in their control and the things that are in the control of others

- Focus corporate resources and energies on things that are in their control and steer away from things that aren't in their control

- Be prepared to disengage from failing projects—projects that come up against parameters the organization doesn't control

- Be prepared to share responsibility for failing projects, setting aside personal egos

RULE **5**

"Always embrace the truth."
—ANTISTHENES

Anyone who has worked for a large organization has probably noticed a herdlike mentality among subordinates—a tendency to routinely endorse the decisions made at the top, even if those decisions steer the corporate ship in the wrong direction. Dishonest assessments and false praise are potentially toxic features of the corporate environment and must be dealt with in a straightforward manner by the genuine leader. "Apple-polishing" is distortive of truth, and truth is the lifeblood of the organization.

> Effective leaders should always embrace the truth, always encourage candid criticism throughout the organization, be skeptical of flattering appraisals, and never let authority place a wedge between them and the truth.

The roster of famous intellectuals residing in sixth- and fourth-century Athens is long indeed. Not the least among these noted thinkers was an Athenian named Antisthenes (circa 450–360 BC). As a young man, Antisthenes had studied with the great sophist master Gorgias but eventually became a devoted member of the Socratic circle and is often identified as one of the founding members of the Cynic School. None of his numerous works have survived in entirety, but a few pithy fragments have come down to us from antiquity. Among these is the following:

"There are only two people who will tell you the truth about yourself—an enemy who has lost his temper and a friend who loves you dearly." Here again, we encounter a truism that defies the specificities of time and place. Antisthenes' message, that the evaluative commentaries offered by those around us must be viewed with considerable skepticism, is a keen insight with a variety of important implications for the modern manager. In general terms, it highlights the remarkable infrequency with which people receive legitimate appraisals about themselves. By extension, Antisthenes' quote also raises questions about how one should react to the rare speaker of truth as well as to the majority whose words are less than fully candid. It is specifically these latter points that must be considered with great care by those in authority.

How a leader responds in these situations will disclose not only that person's likely success as an administrator but, more fundamentally, the leader's status as a person. And, as we have argued throughout, it is the quality of the latter that ultimately determines the functionality and worth of the former.

As a rule, business organizations are rarely inclined to examine their own premises. Instead, people are routinely expected, if not compelled, to endorse the prevailing system of beliefs. While this approach may appear useful in terms of maintaining cultural harmony, in truth it constitutes a serious threat to the organization's general health and well-being because no organization can benefit from having mechanically endorsed views serve as authoritative norms. It is imperative, therefore, that leaders continuously ratify cultural premises and that skeptics and contrarians be given pride of place in the process.

Wise leaders, the men and women who possess genuine insight about administrative life, understand that honest assessment is an essential requirement of effective leadership. In the absence of such assessment, it is next to impossible to formulate accurate and effective policy. It is crucial, therefore, that opportunity for candid expression be encouraged as widely as possible throughout the organization. However, there seems to be an inverse correlation between level of authority and level of truth. In other words, the higher up the corporate ladder an executive ascends, the less likely it is that person will receive complete and accurate evaluation.

Above all, it is highly unlikely that any subordinate will candidly challenge the executive's decision making—no matter how legitimate that criticism might be. Encouraging to whatever degree such submissiveness on the part of subordinates jeopardizes the welfare of both the organization and the leader.

- Be skeptical of complimentary appraisals.
- Encourage candid expression throughout the organization.
- Understand that effective leadership requires honest assessment.
- Don't let authority distance you from the truth.
- Always welcome candid criticism.

None of what has been stated thus far qualifies as esoteric insight. Anyone with even a modest administrative background understands the virtue of honest appraisal. The difficulty lies in resisting powerful tendencies that point in the opposite direction. For example, is it possible to imagine anyone who actually welcomes criticism? Is it not the case that when it comes to accepting disapproval, we all tend to be more than a bit thin-skinned? Are executives somehow exempt from these tendencies or is it the case that corporate high achievers may actually be more inclined toward adverse reaction than most other individuals? Remember, these are men and women who are used to success, used to giving orders, used to being right. They are not in the habit of being told their policies are ill-advised. Given these dispositions the obvious question becomes, to what degree is a leader willing and able to suppress the need for applause in favor of encouraging institutionally fortifying candor?

The answer to these questions is simple. Real leaders make a frequent practice of soliciting honest appraisal from subordinates, and they do so because they understand that the word "truth" is not some abstract notion sought by starry-eyed dreamers. Truth is the lifeblood of a well-run organization, and it is also an administrator's best ally in obtaining organizational goals.

Unfortunately, there are few administrators who have the psychological wherewithal to conduct themselves in this manner. Few have the maturity and emotional security to accept criticism.

As a result, the majority tend to create environments in which lots of lip service is paid to free and open inquiry but everyone understands that the term "truth" comes with a warning label that reads, "Express at your own risk." Is there any doubt that this kind of bad faith between manager and staff can have lethal effects upon the organization? Is there any question that tolerance for genuine truth is one of the key features distinguishing a real leader from a mere supervisor?

Real leaders:

- Solicit honest appraisals from subordinates
- Understand that truth is the lifeblood of a well-run organization
- Tolerate and encourage genuine criticism

Let us now examine a few of the classic maneuvers by which administrative personnel discourage truth and set the stage thereby for the proliferation of yes-men and bootlickers.

Imagine that an executive assistant's position has recently become available at a major electronics corporation. The executive for whom the new employee will work plans to personally conduct the last round of interviews, which will involve three final candidates, and has informed HR of that decision. One of these individuals appears to be particularly well qualified, in terms of both credentials and prior work experience. During the interview this individual comes across as pleasant, confident, and well informed but at one point during the session disagrees with a position taken by his potential boss. The candidate's remarks are in no way disrespectful or argumentative. They are presented in a businesslike manner along with supportive evidence to reinforce the premise. At the conclusion of the interview cycle, the executive informs HR that the lead candidate has been disqualified on the grounds of being opinionated and quarrelsome.

Another illustration of the same intolerance for honesty involves the important issue of executive access. Many managers are strongly disinclined to allow those with contrary opinions meaningful opportunity to express their views. Imagine the following situation: As an outspoken subordinate enters the boss's office a cleverly arranged signal is offered the secretary; she knows to buzz the executive out of the meeting within the next ten minutes. In other words, little or no time will be extended to disagreeable truth. On the other hand, those who sing the praises of the same executive are lavishly extended time to do so. These toadies are allowed to clutter the executive's calendar on a habitual basis. There is always room in the schedule for their servile songs.

Finally, let's consider the case of an affable staff member who is more adept at ingratiating himself with superiors than he is at performing his job. Time and again, this individual is responsible for botched projects and failed opportunities. Yet somehow, while others with similar track records are summarily dismissed, this person remains firmly entrenched in his position. Apparently, skilled fawning trumps incompetence in such cases. Given the manager's need of, and affection for, servile flattery, this incapable rascal enjoys a unique job security.

Other staff members are as outraged as they are demoralized by this travesty of corporate accountability.

How pseudo-leaders seal themselves off from truth:

- They avoid hiring heretics— "opinionated" and "quarrelsome" individuals.

- They have little time for dissenting opinions in corporate meetings.

- They evaluate subordinates according to their affability rather than their performance.

To one degree or another, each of these three cases demonstrates the wisdom contained in Antisthenes' aphorism. Candid assessments are rare and precious things that should never be taken for granted. It is necessary, therefore, that managers develop the skill and the courage to carefully read the motives of those around them.

Now, when it comes to distinguishing the fawning hypocrite from an individual who legitimately concurs with a supervisor's opinions we readily admit there are no facile recipes, crystal balls, or tea leaves ready for reading. One might, however, perform the following diagnostic test. The supervisor could offer a series of viewpoints contrary to the ones actually held. These stated positions should be clearly misguided and potentially inimical to organizational interests. If, under these circumstances, the subordinate continues to obsequiously endorse the lender's insincere proposals, then clearly this is a yes-man or -woman who should never be taken as a credible source of truth.

As effective as such an experiment might prove to be, the more powerful mechanism for revealing duplicitous flatterers relates to the unifying thread that runs throughout this entire work, which is that "knowing thyself" is the critical competency that illumines virtually every aspect of administrative life, including the ability to accurately unveil subordinate motives. Those who have looked deeply into themselves enjoy certain tacit understandings and insights that facilitate looking deeply into others. In other words, learning to stop conning oneself will place the manager in a substantially better position to recognize others' attempts at conning.

While it is appropriate that every individual give at least some consideration to these points, they are of particular significance for those who would claim the mantle of leadership. No leader can hope to do a responsible job in an atmosphere devoid of opportunity for candid expression and forthright analysis. Which is to say, real leaders clearly recognize that there is no greater organizational asset than unencumbered truth. And with this understanding in mind, the genuine leader will never be surrounded with a company of honey-tongued parasites, never limit the lines of communication to those who passively accept the predigested views of management, never make personnel decisions based on an assumed capacity to program or control a potential employee, and never make the utterance of truth the organization's one unpardonable sin. Simply put, the encouragement of fresh and innovative thinking, what might be termed "managed heresy," is an essential aspect of enlightened leadership.

With regard to encouraging such heresy, the real challenge lies in establishing a proper balance between ossified thinking on the one hand and radical unorthodoxy on the other. Clearly, timeworn and uninspired thinking can imperil an organization's very existence, but so can extremist innovations that bear little or no relationship to reality. What organizations must seek, therefore, is that fertile middle ground between tried-and-true approaches that may have become too tame and realistic innovations that offer meaningful prospects of benefit.

One way to accomplish this is to have the organization sponsor a quarterly contest in which employees are encouraged to think outside the box. All suggestions, including the eccentric and fanciful, are officially solicited and reviewed. The evaluations are conducted by a panel of senior executives. This screening mechanism will allow management an opportunity to control, direct, and refine the "heresies" as needed. It will also afford a valuable diagnostic opportunity for management to gauge the mood and disposition of staff members in the matter of change. Winning propositions might be awarded cash prizes and a spot on the Vanguard Plaque honoring unconventional thinkers. Authors of declined proposals are provided a detailed explanation for the rejection along with encouragement to continue in their idiosyncratic ways.

Nurture a culture of free and candid expression:

- Encourage critical and innovative thinking throughout the organization.

- Hire a heretic or two.

- Remember that it's better to be surrounded by heretics than by apple-polishers.

In the end, the long-term success of any institution is intimately connected to the good name and sound reputation the organization enjoys. However, the integrity of an organization is only as good as the integrity of its leadership. If, therefore, the leaders of an institution are inclined to deny, manipulate, and manufacture their own version of truth, if they are only capable of accepting some sanitized notion of that term reflecting their own narrow insecurities, then they will never be in a position to adequately advance the organization's well-being. Moreover, they will never own the right to be called "real" leaders.

THE GOLDEN LEADERSHIP GRID

- Truth is an invaluable corporate asset. Don't let it go to waste. Embrace it.

- Be skeptical of members who routinely endorse and praise your decisions.

- Hire a "heretic" or two and let them speak their minds, even if they are critical of your decisions.

- Foster a culture conducive to honest appraisal of corporate strategies and policies.

RULE **6**

"Let competition reveal talent."
—HESIOD

T alent is the catchword of modern business, for good reason. It is the ultimate source of competitive advantage, especially in high-technology industries where corporations rely on innovation to differentiate themselves from the competition.

> While knowledgeable employees can be hired in the marketplace or recruited from within, bringing their talent out and aligning it with organizational interests requires an environment that allows employees to compete with each other in a constructive rather than a destructive way.

In addition, managers must carefully select subordinates who evidence potential to prosper in a competitive setting, individuals in whom "contest" is likely to engender high levels of enthusiasm and creativity.

Anyone familiar with the history of ancient Greece knows that conflict was a continuous aspect of their civilization. Few people in the history of humankind have been more prone to bear arms against themselves, more inclined to deny themselves the blessings of peace, than the ancient Greeks. Needless to say, the reasons for this internecine conflict are highly complex, but historians have long noted a powerful competitive instinct at the heart of Greek civilization which, in both its depth and diffusion, suggests a unique cultural trait. The Greek term for these rivalrous passions is *agon*—"contest"—and it seems that from the earliest beginnings of their history the Greeks employed competition as a mechanism for identifying an individual's comparative worth and merit. Specifically, they understood the potent psychological forces involved in opportunities to achieve distinctions of honor and glory. It may even be the case that much of the Greek cultural achievement was directly related to the harnessing of these energies.

This agonistic spirit is traceable in virtually every facet of ancient Greek society; the athletic games were merely one of its more obvious manifestations. One of the most interesting descriptions of how the Greeks perceived this competitive impulse is found in the verse of a poet named Hesiod, one of the most highly regarded figures in ancient literature, who discusses the effects of human friction in terms remarkably consistent with the principles of modern capitalist doctrine.

Hesiod was an epic poet who lived in Boeotia (central Greece) in the late eighth century BC. He is noted primarily for two poems, *Theogony* and *Works and Days*. It is the latter work that concerns us here because in this poem Hesiod describes two forms of *Eris* (strife) that animate the human spirit. One is a malignant force that promotes a "rough strife" resulting in all the evils we associate with war. Here Hesiod refers to the sorrowful discord that stained the pages of Greek history with so much blood. Yet, Hesiod also acknowledges another, more beneficial and productive form of strife. This form of contention is the child of envy and pride, but it does not lead to the grim brutalities of the battlefield. Rather, its impact tends to be productive for all concerned in specifically economic terms.

Hesiod explains how this benign version of *Eris* motivates the shiftless man to work. He speaks of how neighbor vies with neighbor in the pursuit of wealth and how members of every vocation are motivated to compete against others in their field. The net effect of this competitive spirit is the production of more and better "fruit," and it is for this reason that Hesiod speaks of how "This strife is wholesome for men."

Antagonism	Competition
Destructive strife	Constructive strife
Releases the selfishness of the individual	Releases the ingenuity and creativity of the individual

Although Hesiod composed his poetry many centuries ago, he nevertheless seems to comprehend that critical connection between human ego and economic productivity. Long before John Locke, Adam Smith, or David Ricardo, this ancient poet recognized ways in which competitive energies might contribute to material prosperity. In many respects, this is the same basic logic that continues to drive our economic system today. Although the competitors are no longer the potters and peasant farmers described by Hesiod but enormous corporations controlling billions of dollars in assets, the fundamental premises remain the same, namely that people have an innate competitive instinct that pushes them to seek achievements beyond those of their compatriots. Both the strength of this energy as well as its benefits are clearly demonstrated by the material accomplishments of the system we call capitalism. And it goes without saying that nurturing, harnessing, directing these energies is a major test of those who would leave their mark as real leaders.

The challenge involved here is more complex than it might appear initially. The leader must design strategies capable of accessing that potentially productive reservoir of passions and sentiments that lie within every human being. In order to accomplish this task effectively, and more specifically, in order to link these powers to the achievement of organizational objectives, the leader must be a keen assessor of human personality.

Here again, we remind the reader of the thematic constant that runs throughout this entire narrative: self-understanding is the key precondition of understanding others. Every real leader knows that in personnel management, "knowing thyself" is a critical asset whose absence greatly complicates the task of tapping into the motivational energies of subordinates. Among other things, a clear and honest understanding of oneself will significantly reduce distortive tendencies when it comes to analyzing the work potentials of staff members. For example, a leader will need to identify which subordinates are best able to accept new competitive challenges. Are there some staff members less well suited to contest-oriented approaches? Are there others who might use competitive opportunity in a disruptive and counterproductive manner? Arriving at answers to these questions requires a variety of subtle psychological insights, including those relating to the leader's own character and personality.

How to nurture competition:

- Be a keen assessor of human personality—including your own

- Identify subordinates who are receptive to competitive challenges

- Avoid utilizing subordinates who can turn competition into antagonism

With these premises in mind, we can now consider a hypothetical situation illustrating the salutary effects of Hesiod's constructive strife. Let us imagine that a major corporation needs to devise the most effective means of promoting a new product line. The unit in charge of advertising is divided in terms of how best to structure the campaign. One group feels the best plan would be to draw a series of aggressive comparisons between the new product and similar items available from the competition. Another group within the advertising division believes a better method of promotion would be a campaign stressing the corporation's long-acknowledged status as a trusted industry leader. In response to these divergent views, the manager decides upon a tactic sometimes referred to as "creative tension." The advertising team is divided into two subunits reflecting the two different approaches. Both groups are tasked with creating a detailed campaign, which will then be submitted to senior management for final evaluation. The winning project will form the centerpiece of a national campaign. The leadership is careful to present the plans in competitive terms, as a kind of *agon* between Team A and Team B. Team members are made aware of special financial incentives earmarked for members of the winning group. In addition, word of the "contest" is vigorously promoted throughout the organization.

Over time, this promotion creates a certain buzz within the company with the result that the project takes on a special status. Team members begin to recognize that this is not simply another job assignment. Increasingly, they understand that the entire organization is watching and waiting to see the outcome of this rivalry. As a result, team members invest the operation with degrees of time, effort, and creative commitment rarely seen. As the process continues, those involved become more and more engaged on a personal level. Success is no longer about securing a bonus check. It becomes a matter of esteem, rank, reputation, and personal pride. In the end, the winning campaign goes on to become a smashing success, illustrating the benefits an organization stands to receive by accessing the agonistic energies of its personnel.

While imaginary, the foregoing scenario contains an important life lesson: Human ambition, when properly managed, can play a critical role in fulfilling organizational objectives. Implicit in all this is a distinction between workers who simply punch the clock—mechanically conform to their daily work requirements—and personnel who are deeply committed to achieving exceptional levels of job performance. The former are content with mere compliance while the later define success in terms of a personal standard whose criteria exceed those mandated by the organization. Motivation of this sort, what we might call "impulsions from within," is an all-too-rare phenomenon in large, complex institutions. Nevertheless, such motivation must be made a pivotal concern of any real leader because failure to tap into motivations of this kind means the organization is denied any real ability to achieve its full potential.

The Antagonistic Worker	The Competitive Worker
Committed to mere conformity and mediocrity	Deeply committed to innovation and excellence
Impulsion from without— content to merely meet company performance standards	Impulsion from within— striving to exceed company-set performance standards

As we've already suggested, the challenge to securing this degree of worker dedication is no simple matter. Among a long list of key variables are the following: The leader must carefully select the right people for the competitive task; must properly incentivize the activity; must devise strategies that will encourage those involved to embrace the project on a personal basis; must see to it that the competition does not lead to permanent enmity and division; and, finally, must ensure that the vanquished receive a meaningful share of acknowledgment and praise.

There is little question that worker motivation is a critical component of organizational success. The only real issue is whether or not an institution is actually receiving the commitment it deserves from its workers. In too many instances, companies command only a fraction of the dedication they require from employees. One of the most effective ways of reversing this tendency is to forge a meaningful union between worker motivation and organizational interests, and one of the best ways to accomplish that is to ignite the fires of competition. Those who succeed in harnessing these remarkable energies first described by Hesiod will not only advance the objectives and purposes of the organization but also go far in distinguishing themselves as real leaders.

THE GOLDEN LEADERSHIP GRID

- As is the case in society at large, corporations are prone to antagonism (a destructive strife) and competition (a constructive strife). It is the task of the leader to ignite the fires of competition and extinguish the fires of antagonism.

- Identify the subordinates who espouse the spirit of competition; always seek excellence and encourage competition that advances the cause of the organization.

- Avoid subordinates who settle for mediocrity and have a tendency to antagonize each other, threatening to turn the organization into a collection of disruptive, warring fiefdoms.

RULE 7

"Live life by a higher code."
—ARISTOTLE

Of all challenges business leaders face as corporate organizations grow in size and diversity, one stands out above the others: the proper alignment of subordinates' behaviors, goals, interests, and attitudes with those of the larger organization. Without such alignment, leaders direct in name only. They have the authority, but not the power to lead effectively. Subordinates may comply with leadership decisions publicly but violate them privately, with the result that institutional objectives are far less likely to be achieved.

Under these circumstances, it comes as no surprise that scores of academic papers have been published proposing all sorts of solutions to the problem, from bureaucratic restructuring to sanctions and rewards to cultural controls. But none of these measures can yield the desired results unless leaders earn the trust of their subordinates. The trouble is that trust doesn't happen by accident. An army of consultants cannot build it. Trust must be nurtured over time, and it comes only to those who have dedicated themselves to a higher life code. This is the means by which subordinates become committed followers.

Dedicate yourself to a higher standard of personal conduct; don't hold grudges and ill will toward those who offend; be ready to assist those who are in need without

(continued)

asking something in return; remain calm in the face of crisis; dedicate yourself to principle without compromise; earn the trust, respect, and admiration of your subordinates through your character, not through the authority conferred upon you by the corporate chart; turn authority into power.

In the history of Western thought few voices can match the authoritative tones of Aristotle—which accounts for Dante's reference to him as "The master of those who know." In both the range of his inquiries and the depth of his many insights, Aristotle ranks as one of the greatest thinkers who ever lived. By way of demonstration, one need only consult the work titled *Nicomachean Ethics*, in which Aristotle presents a detailed account of the moral and rational elements requisite for human happiness. In Book 4 of that text Aristotle offers a famous portrait of the so-called "magnanimous man." Our word "magnanimous" stems from the Latin term *mangnanimitas*, referring to noble or lofty sentiment. The original Greek, however, uses the more expressive phrase *megalopsuchia*, meaning "great-souled."

Much of the description offered for this individual illustrates the many distinctions separating ancient and modern worldviews. There are, however, certain features of the "great-souled" person's character and bearing that remain worthy of modern consideration and, more specifically, remarkably relevant for the question of leadership. Indeed, as we shall see, one might even argue that those devoid of these magnanimous attributes can never really enjoy the status of genuine leader.

What then are the defining characteristics of the person Aristotle describes as "great-souled"? What is clear from the outset of Aristotle's presentation is the strong sense of self-worth felt by the great-souled individual. At first glance this attitude may suggest an egoistic or self-absorbed person, but a careful reading of Aristotle's narrative indicates nothing of the sort. The magnanimous man or woman is not a narcissist. Whatever sense of self-satisfaction this individual might feel is entirely merited to the extent he or she lives by a higher and more rigorous life code than does the average person. In other words, distinctive men and women are entitled to an elevated sense of self, but it is precisely because they have organized their lives in loyalty to a higher standard that they will not demean themselves by engaging in immodest or conceited behavior. When it comes to the great-souled individual personal honor, not ego, is the ultimate priority and concern.

With this general premise in mind, we are free to ask how an elevated life code translates into actual conduct. For one thing, Aristotle makes clear that the magnanimous person is invariably a morally attuned individual. As such, he or she is never tempted by the petty vanities that impassion and misguide most people. Things such as money, power, and title are viewed by the great-souled with a profound sense of indifference. In the end, the magnanimous man or woman might well obtain such things but not as a result of some dishonorable attempt at their acquisition.

Rather, the accumulation of these assets result from the quality and substance of who and what the magnanimous individual is as a person. In other words, it is the life code itself, a code that has as its priority a principled and dignified existence that results in the attainment of these secondary concerns.

Magnanimous men and women:

- Are morally astute individuals
- Resist the temptation of petty vanities that impassion and misguide most people
- Are indifferent to status distinctions of money, power, and titles

Along these same lines, Aristotle discusses the relationship between the great-souled and those less high-minded. There is no question that magnanimous individuals fully appreciate their own superiority in all such interactions. But at the same time they are completely disinclined to flaunt their own preeminence. To draw negative comparisons, to demean or debase another person, would completely violate the standard by which superior men and women conduct themselves. Such behavior would, in effect, go far toward invalidating any claim to elevated status. Accordingly, those who are truly magnanimous have neither need for, nor interest in, burnishing their own ego at the expense of others.

In describing the great-souled person's communicative style, Aristotle makes reference to an unyielding concern for truth. Magnanimous people are much less concerned about the opinion of others than they are about honesty. Accordingly, such individuals are disinclined to choreograph their words. They speak directly without calculation or guile, and as result all of their communications reveal a full and unvarnished description of both sentiment and intentions.

Duplicity, in either word or deed, is completely inconsistent with the level of moral nobility suggested by Aristotle's use of the term "great-souled."

Other characteristic features of those possessed of magnanimous spirit include a refusal to hold grudges or harbor ill will toward those who offend, a ready willingness to assist those in need matched by a strong disinclination to seek aid in return, and a consistent ability to remain calm and untroubled in the face of crisis. Where others react with fear and misgiving, the great-souled individual's composure remains unshaken.

In sum, the person identified by Aristotle as "magnanimous" is a man or woman of unusually high moral stature. As a result, these individuals are dedicated to a life code that distinguishes them from the mass of humanity. Their standards and priorities tend to reflect one overarching concern—the maintenance of personal integrity—and it is precisely for this reason that such individuals can be legitimately spoken of as "great-souled." Whereas others rapidly succumb to moral compromise, those who are magnanimous reject such conduct as beneath their personal dignity and, as such, unworthy of consideration. In short, a person deserving of the designation "great-souled" lives an unusually principled life governed by an appropriate sense of pride and a dutiful commitment to personal virtue.

Magnanimous people:

- Live by a higher life code that distinguishes and sets them apart from the mass of humanity

- Maintain personal integrity

- Never submit to moral compromise

It remains to spell out the implications of Aristotle's portrait of the *megalopsuchia* for modern management. Perhaps the best way to accomplish this task is to begin by reminding the reader that every large, complex social system has in fact two identities. First, there is the formal organization, all of the official structures and lines of authority typically indicated by the organization chart. Second, there is the informal organization, which isn't reflected by the organization chart: worker attitudes, perceptions, and judgments that play a vital role in determining the success or failure of corporate enterprise. Too often, leaders tend to neglect the power and influence of informal organization. They assume that personnel will automatically comply with the "system" as demanded by the institution's formal authorities. What is not understood here is the potential for employees to obey the letter of formal policy while remaining violative of its spirit. In other words, the informal organization tends to have a mind of its own, and its loyalties and commitments are not automatically guaranteed simply because a policy is proclaimed from above.

We are not suggesting that the informal organization has a tendency to overtly violate organizational directives.

No, the phenomenon we are describing here is far more complex and subtle than that. It involves the very real danger of a merely mechanical compliance on the part of staff personnel—in other words, staff members meeting their contractual obligations and nothing more. The difference between companies that remain continuously profitable, that enjoy the benefits of cutting-edge innovation, and that distinguish themselves as leaders in their fields versus those that merely exist at the margin is the dedicated involvement and commitment of the informal organization. Winning organizations understand that ardent workers are not created by corporate mandate but are instead the result of a certain quality of leadership.

Formal Organization	Informal Organization
"The system," as determined by the organization chart	"The system," as perceived by the members of the organization
Sets the public agenda of the organization	Sets the private agendas of individual members

In relating these premises to leadership it is first necessary to consider the distinction between authority and power. Authority is something conferred by the formal organization that entitles a manager to make decisions, resolve disputes, and direct subordinates. In order to reinforce these prerogatives, those who receive authority are often invested with the symbols of office indicating privileged status, such as a reserved parking space or keys to the executive washroom.

Power, on the other hand, is a notion broader than that of officially assigned authority. It involves a general capacity to influence the beliefs and conduct of others even without formal title. It is often the case that those lacking formal authority nevertheless command considerable amounts of power.

Indeed, under some circumstances subordinates can actually enjoy more tangible influence than do their superiors. The explanation for this is found in the distinction presented earlier in this chapter between the formal and informal organization. The former is in a position to specify those in authority while the latter tends to determine who has actual power. In fact, in strictly operational terms, it may not be too much to suggest that staff members have a de facto ability to determine who the real players will be in almost any organization. In light of all this, it is essential that institutions seek to invest authority in those who also enjoy the power bestowed by the informal organization.

Without this convergence of authority and power one can count on neither effective leadership nor the achievement of company objectives.

But how does one go about identifying those who might effectively combine the support of both the formal and informal aspects of the organization? On this issue, one need look no further than the pages of Aristotle's *Nicomachean Ethics*. Specifically, the

Authority	Power
A narrow and formal description of the decision-making tree, as determined by the organization chart	A broad and informal definition of the decision-making tree
Reinforced with prerogatives, office labels, and title	Involves the general capacity to influence the beliefs and conduct of others even without formal title

figure described there as the magnanimous man or woman is a model candidate for the fruitful marriage of authority and power.

In this regard, the real challenge lies not in investing some executive with formal authority but in identifying a person capable of earning the respect and admiration of the informal organization.

A review of the defining characteristics of the magnanimous man or woman provides a suggestive image of who that individual is likely to be. Imagine a person whose dedication to principle knows no compromise. A model colleague—trustworthy, candid, loath to engage in any conduct that might be interpreted as dishonorable; a person for whom the priority is maintaining a personal standard of integrity rather than scoring points on behalf of career advancement.

Consider the influential reputation such a person would inevitably enjoy within the organization. Consider, too, the potential such an individual might have to shape the opinions and motivations of coworkers. Now consider what impact this same man or woman could have if, in addition to these personal qualities, that person were also officially endowed with authority. Imagine a leader who enjoyed the enthusiastic backing of both the formal and informal sides of the organization. Wouldn't this joint endorsement ensure the very highest probability of institutional success?

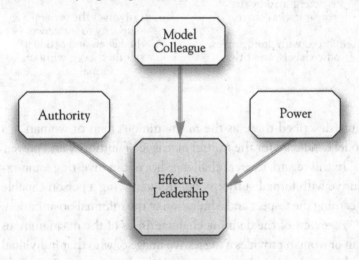

The implications of all this for a properly informed notion of leadership should be clear. Real leadership has little to do with the trappings of authority. An executive might occupy a lavish and much sought-after office but still not have any meaningful capacity to lead. The reason for this, as we have suggested throughout, is related to factors of character and personality that no official title can confer. Executives who succeed in clawing their way to the top but do so in an unprincipled manner inevitably have their deficiencies revealed over time. This, because they are unable to secure the trust, respect, and admiration of their subordinates—all of which real leaders understand is essential. It is for this reason that all legitimate leaders correspond, to one degree or another, with Aristotle's portrait of the magnanimous man or woman. On some level of their managerial consciousness they understand that a reputation for personal integrity is an invaluable asset in the administrative economy of any institution.

Moreover, they recognize that such reputations are unique statuses granted only to those who have dedicated themselves to a higher standard of personal conduct. In short, they appreciate the fact that there is both wisdom and utility to be found in highmindedness. It should surprise no one, therefore, that some of the most successful leaders in some of the most successful corporations are not simply well informed about product development or market dynamics. They are, above all, well informed about themselves. And for those who believe that corporate ends justify the means, no matter how illicit those means may be, we suggest that the proceeds of cunning and duplicity can never match the ripened benefits of integrity—a point fully understood by real leaders and one lost upon those disinclined to live life by a higher code.

Admittedly this all sounds well and good, but what of a situation in which a manager finds it impossible to maintain personal integrity and still be seen as an asset in the eyes of stockholders and senior executives? No one can deny that dissonance such as this can easily arise in the workplace. Although each situation is unique to a given context, we nevertheless offer the following general guideline. Given the competitive nature of the business environment, moral rigidity is neither practical nor desirable. Salaries are not extended to managers so they can sit front and center in the church choir. Accordingly, those who stubbornly deny the realistic dictates of level-headed pragmatism need to be disabused of their moralistic pretensions. If, however, the only way to satisfy shareholders is to fundamentally realign one's moral compass, to compromise core values and principles, then it may be time to dust off the resume.

The wisdom of exploring vocational alternatives under these circumstances can be traced to two sources. First, one should ask, what is the likely future of a disreputable business enterprise? Morally tainted institutions always seem to forget that there are inevitable penalties for perfidy—who wants to do business with Babylon? Second, those who have made personal integrity a hallmark feature of their lives, those who stand for something and who understand the real value of things, should never allow anyone or anything to tarnish such an achievement. Organizations worth working for understand that men and women who abide by higher codes are invaluable assets they can ill afford to be without.

THE GOLDEN LEADERSHIP GRID

- Understand the formal and informal structure of your organization.

- Realize that effective leadership requires command over both the formal and the informal organization.

- Supervising the formal organization is the easy part, as the organization chart sets the lines of authority and grants the leader official status.

- Directing the informal organization is the difficult part, as formal management status cannot guarantee that subordinates comply privately with executive decisions.

- What can warrant such compliance is the integrity of your character, a higher code of life that turns subordinates into faithful followers. Are you worthy of their loyalties?

RULE 8

"Always evaluate information with a critical eye."
—THE SKEPTICS

When it comes to assessing information, no organization can afford to be complacent. For one thing, knowledge and information are in a constant state of change given technological advancements. As a result, what may have been conventional wisdom yesterday is no longer valid today. In addition, capable leaders understand that they must consider the circumstances that shaped the information. Even the means by which the information is conveyed must be critically examined. Leaders should never assume that the information they receive is unsoiled by hidden agendas or political objectives. Accordingly, leaders must suspend judgment until the data has been critically evaluated.

> Don't rely upon old premises, assertions, and theories. Develop a critical mindset that accepts nothing at face value, certify the credibility and usefulness of critical information, analyze the context that produces critical information and the messengers that convey it, and never rush to judgments.

Anyone familiar with the spirit and method of ancient Greek philosophy understands that open-ended inquiry was its unique hallmark and that it was specifically this willingness to pursue truth in a fresh and unrestricted manner that distinguished the Greeks from the rest of antiquity.

Whereas other ancient peoples were burdened by the limitations of received opinion, the Greeks insisted, as Socrates said, that "the unexamined life is not worth living." Over time, however, even Greek thought became encrusted with a variety of dogmatic assumptions that were inconsistent with the truth-seeking foundations of its culture.

Eventually, these undemonstrated convictions were challenged by a philosophical movement known as Skepticism, which rejected the knowledge assertions of the dogmatists. Although the Skeptics did not constitute a recognizable group until the third century BC, when they assumed control of the Academy at Athens, the foundations of skepticism were themselves a deeply embedded feature of Greek philosophy. From its inception the tendency to doubt and question was a characteristic feature of ancient philosophical tradition. Its rudiments can be found at least as far back as the pre-Socratic speculation of Heraclitus and Xenophanes and is more clearly evident among sophist thinkers such as Protagoras and Gorgias. Above all, however, it is Socrates who must be acknowledged as primarily responsible for reminding us that we must be vigilant against the conceits of wisdom, that we are all strongly inclined to assume we understand things that in truth we fail to genuinely comprehend. This position explains Socrates' famous response to the Oracle of Delphi's identification of him as the wisest of the Greeks: "All that I know is that I know nothing." In other words, Socrates is most wise precisely because he is not inflated with the pretensions of knowledge.

Don't Be Inflated with the Pretensions of Knowledge

- Be vigilant against the conceits of knowledge.
- Always question the things you are inclined to take for granted.
- Know the qualitative limitations of knowledge.

It is this general logic that was adopted by the Skeptics and made the fundamental guideline of their battle against baseless intellectual conviction. In the process of pressing their attack, the Skeptics advanced a critical mental attitude that they believed needed to become a standard feature of every thinking person's cognitive arsenal. The essence of this critical mindset is reflected in the ancient term *epoche*, which refers to a bracketing or "suspension of judgment."

What the Skeptics were highlighting in their advocacy of this concept was a need to control an almost reflexive tendency to jump to conclusions, to assign truth status to ideas, theories, and explanations that fail to merit such attribution.

Their alternative was a probabilistic conception of truth offered as an antidote to dubious certainty.

Say, for example, an organization is developing a new product, which must be brought to market in the next twelve months. The ancient Skeptics would insist the following sorts of questions be posed: What is the probability the R & D unit will complete its work on schedule; what is the probability we will be the first to unveil this new technology; What is the probability the product will secure the needed additional 5 percent of market share? The virtue of this approach lies in its capacity to temper assumptions of special insight by continually affirming the tentative nature of knowledge claims. Specifically, it offers a calculus dedicated to producing more caution and less conviction, which may in turn help establish the wisdom of contingency thinking (that is, Plan B)—something every real leader should have readily available. In short, skeptics advise that the possibilities of certainty are more complex and more elusive than we tend to imagine and, as a result, considerable caution must be exercised against rushing to judgment. Although these ideas may be traceable to a philosophical movement more than two thousand years old, they remain well worth our consideration today; in particular, they offer a critically important premise for modern managers.

Develop a Critical Mindset

- Don't rush to conclusions.
- Always reexamine conventional ideas, theories, and explanations.
- Understand that certainty is more elusive than we tend to assume.

By adopting the cautionary message contained in skepticism's idea of *epoche*, contemporary leaders stand to substantially enhance their administrative effectiveness. For one thing, the idea of "bracketing" or temporarily isolating some bit of information has the beneficial effect of decelerating the process by which information is endorsed. Rather than extend data an automatic stamp of approval, the information is segregated and made an object of critical evaluation.

By inspecting the data in this manner, by holding it up to the light, so to speak, a leader is able to certify the credibility and usefulness of the information prior to its inclusion in the decision-making process. Ideally speaking, all policy formation should proceed along these lines, but in truth the counsels of the ancient Skeptics are rarely heeded by most modern policy makers. All too often, important choices are based upon improperly examined premises, premises based more on conceptual inertia than on meticulous assessment. Any leader who has experienced the consequences of failed policy knows by benefit of hindsight how vitally important it is to have a realistic understanding of a policy's operational assumptions. If these suppositions are false, if they are based upon accustomed ways of thinking without the benefit of critical reflection, then the policy has little prospect of real success. In short, it is important to acknowledge that dogmatic assumption is not a malady unique to philosophers. Large organizations are just as capable of advancing propositions and viewpoints devoid of legitimate factual foundation. The astute leader understands all this and proceeds cautiously when it comes to certifying the credibility of data essential to the task of decision making. He or she recognizes that the risks of corporate dogmatism are very real and that they have the potential to misdirect policy, thereby radically reducing the prospects for institutional success.

In addition to reminding us of the dangers inherent in dogmatic assertions, the ancient Skeptics were also advancing a more wide-ranging counsel: the formation of a critical habit of mind that accepts nothing at face value. In many respects, this encouragement to doubt, question, and investigate contains an immensely important wisdom that no leader can afford to be without. Here, we are no longer referring to the pitfalls of dogmatic assumption but to a variety of extra-informational variables that often attach themselves to seemingly neutral data.

An important part of the larger message of ancient skepticism is that we need to disabuse ourselves of the myth of pristine information. Much of what we tend to accept as incontrovertibly true and accurate is, in reality, anything but. Both the context and the medium of expression often contain obscure meanings and hidden intentions that are not easily detected at first glance. In this regard, even so-called "hard" evidence such as statistical data needs to be carefully scrutinized. Under certain circumstances numbers too can be made to "dance" in ways that have little connection with objective reality.

An effective leader must, therefore, develop an eye well-practiced in the art of decoding the subtleties of communication. Among the range of issues a leader must be prepared to scrutinize are the source of the information and its likely credibility, the methods by which the data was compiled, the degree to which raw data was processed or filtered by those reporting the information, the institutional track record of the individual or group supplying the data, and the possibility that hidden agendas of a political or psychological nature may have corrupted the data's integrity.

Strictly speaking, no leader can afford to be complacent when it comes to assessing the information needed to operate effectively. In all such cases, the executive must proceed on the assumption that the information received is rarely neutral, objective, or un-soiled by factors that may greatly impede the leader's capacity to arrive at accurate and productive conclusions.

By way of illustration, take Bank of America's acquisition of Countrywide Financial in the middle of the subprime crisis. The purchase of fast-growing mortgage company Countrywide Financial was supposed to be the quick ticket into the mortgage market, a natural area of expansion for a bank with plenty of funds to lend. Instead that purchase was the "poison bait" for Bank of America, and the finance company became the poster child for the excesses of the mortgage market. The problem? Lack of due diligence—nobody bothered to investigate Countrywide's true liabilities. The rest is history.

Handle Critical Information with Skepticism

- Disabuse yourself of the myth of pristine information.

- Always understand the context: the conditions and circumstances that produce critical information.

- Always assess the messengers who convey the information.

The logic of suspending judgment remains powerfully suggestive for modern leaders. Among other things, it reminds us that the assertions, interpretations, and analyses we receive are rarely as true or impartial as they purport to be. Along with many other skills, therefore, it is imperative that the leader also become adept at deciphering the information he or she receives. In addition, it is highly advisable that this same critical mentality be cultivated as widely as possible throughout the organization. Ideally, every institution should seek to create an entire staff of truth testers dedicated to the premise that little if any information can be taken as self-evidently true. If something along these lines can be accomplished, the organization will have gone far toward immunizing itself against the detrimental effects of illusory premises and dogmatic distortions, which is an aspiration every real leader must embrace.

THE GOLDEN LEADERSHIP GRID

- Critical knowledge and information cannot be taken for granted, especially in a rapidly changing world. That's why you must be ready to review information continually.

- Premises, beliefs, fashionable trends, and successful policies are tested every day by reality, and may eventually become irrelevant. That's why you should always maintain an open mind rather than be guided by dogmatic assumptions.

- Critical information is sensitive to the context that produces it, and the messengers who distribute it.

That's why you should develop the habit of closely scrutinizing critical information. Always be mindful of the context, the sources, and the channels from which the information flows.

RULE **9**

"Never underestimate the
power of personal integrity."
—Sophocles

Professional success is the goal of every leader. However, there are two ways to succeed: the easy way and the hard way. The easy way involves a denial of principle and integrity. This approach may yield some rapid, short-term gains, but in the end it typically results in harm to both the organization and the leader. This is because no corporation can benefit when blind ambition and intoxicating greed become the coin of the realm. In the end, the more difficult path represented by ethical conduct will produce superior results for the company and the executive alike.

> Never underestimate the power of personal integrity;
> always set an honorable agenda; adhere to a code of
> professional conduct; never try to justify dishonesty
> and deceit; rather fail with honor than win by cheating.

Along with Aeschylus and Euripides, Sophocles (496–406 BC) was one of the greatest tragic playwrights of classical Greece. While he reportedly wrote 123 dramas, only seven plays have survived. One of these, *Oedipus Rex*, is perhaps the most famous of all the ancient tragedies. It was singled out by no less a figure than Aristotle as the ideal representative of the tragic genre, although it failed to take first prize in the competitions of circa 429 BC.

The plots of Sophocles' dramas are never simple, and one should resist the temptation to reduce them to set patterns or formulas. Typically, they reflect a series of complex interactions between human deficiency on the one hand and obscure divine intentions on the other. Given the fact that the latter are at best dimly perceived by the heroes and heroines of the Greek stage, the result is that peculiar form of suffering we call "tragic." Within this general framework, Sophocles produced a play in 409 BC titled *Philoctetes*, a work we believe should be read and carefully considered by every executive. The two central characters in this drama are Neoptolemus and the famous hero of Troy, Odysseus. From the drama's outset, it is clear these figures are juxtaposed not simply as different personalities but as representatives of entirely distinct life orientations. Neoptolemus is the son of Heracles, perhaps the greatest of all Greek heroes. He is a young man of undefiled principle for whom honor and integrity are the primary concerns of life. By contrast, Odysseus is a man famous for enchanting the souls of others with his wily words. In the ancient literature he is often described as possessing *metis*, meaning "shrewdness" or "craftiness." It should be noted that this term does not imply wisdom or intellectual insight. On the contrary, *metis* suggests the guile and cunning of the fox. In short, Odysseus is a man of mischief and deceit intent upon compromising the youthful integrity of Neoptolemus.

Throughout the play Odysseus advances a dishonorable agenda as old as humanity itself that is cited just as often (perhaps more) today than it was in antiquity. It is the notion that the ends justify the means, that a person is entitled to engage in whatever conduct is necessary in order to accomplish his or her agenda. In other words, one should not allow moral concerns to impede the necessities of practical achievement. In response to this seductive reasoning the young Neoptolemus responds, "I would prefer even to fail with honor than win by cheating."

The Low Road to Success

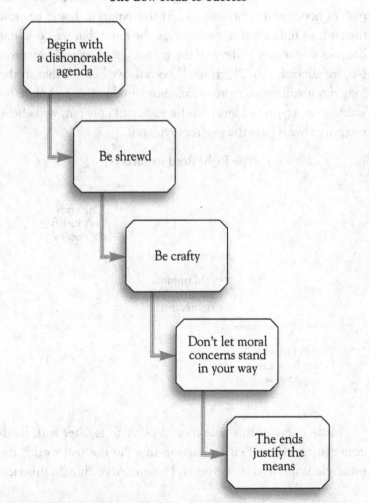

In both word and context, Sophocles' *Philoctetes* succeeds in capturing one of those timeless questions that cynics and idealists have been debating from time immemorial: Which is the proper course in life? Is it the road of least moral resistance, or is it the path of honor and righteousness? At this point, it should be clear the authors unhesitatingly encourage the latter, but we do so not because we naively believe in the efficacy of elves and unicorns. No, we advocate the "high road" because we believe that in the long run it will prove more useful, more productive, and more rewarding on a personal level for the leader. Simply put, we believe integrity always pays the greater dividend.

The Right Road to Success

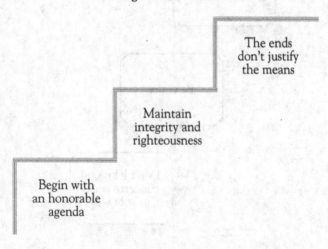

The ends
don't justify
the means

Maintain
integrity and
righteousness

Begin with
an honorable
agenda

Little if any of this reasoning is likely to register with hardcore cynics, given their conviction that "in the real world" the principled path leads to defeat and failure. According to this view success is something that must be grasped by whatever means necessary, and that includes methods devoid of scruple. In fact, it is argued, any executive who allows moral considerations to cloud his or her thinking empowers the competition with potentially devastating advantages. In effect, the cynic argues that the executive is a kind of general who must conduct all business affairs in the spirit of warfare, in which all is fair and permissible. Casualties and collateral damage are simply unavoidable features of combat and must be accepted as part of the costs of doing business.

Something along these lines is the traditional response offered to anyone suggesting a more ethically sensitive approach to administrative life. Our reply to these who invoke this "real world" argument is simply this: dishonesty, duplicity, and deceit are never justifiable activities for a real leader. We understand that some managers have an uncanny ability to rationalize any conduct, no matter how treacherous it might be. But this skill at moral self-deception changes nothing with regard to the impropriety of immoral activities. In fact, it strongly indicates that an executive so inclined has done very little in attempting to follow the dictum to "know thyself." Rather than engage in the hard work of self-understanding, these individuals manufacture a series of fictional rationales that they then endeavor to believe. For those who lack a genuine sense of self, codes of conduct are always situational, fluid, subject to dramatic alteration as circumstances dictate. In short, these individuals lack any meaningful sense of moral norm or standard. Needless to say, these are not enviable qualities for any individual. Moreover, a life strategy such as this typically results in little more than short-term gains because those who routinely allow themselves the cynical convenience of slipping in and out of moral comas will inevitably come to grief in every facet of their life, including their careers.

Real leaders:

- Steer clear of dishonesty, duplicity, and deceit
- Do not try to rationalize unethical conduct
- Don't allow themselves to slip into moral comas

Along these lines, let us compare and contrast the career tracks of two very different administrators. Executive A did not simply climb the corporate ladder, but rather hacked a way to the top in a ruthless manner that resulted in a particularly notorious reputation. From the outset, blind and unlimited ambition determined every decision and judgment that person made. Somewhere along the line Executive A came to believe that "principle" was for losers and that those who foolishly made it an aspect of their professional lives would never be anything more than second-rate leaders. Now in mid-career, this executive was fully persuaded that how high you go depends upon how low you are prepared to sink. Despite the executive's numerous efforts to disguise and deflect many acts of questionable conduct, word has spread that this is an individual not to be trusted.

Initially that view is held almost exclusively by subordinates, but over time even more senior members of the organization begin to understand that there is another side to this person's reputation for "getting the job done." More and more, senior personnel are concerned with a variety of potentially negative consequences associated with entrusting important projects to this individual, ranging from disruptions of corporate morale to legal exposure. The senior VP for human resources speaks for many in the organization in assessing the situation as "most unfortunate" in the sense that this person has obvious ability but is now so tainted ethically as to have become a kind of corporate pariah.

Increasingly, the organization's verdict regarding Executive A is that the individual is a toxic asset, abilities notwithstanding.

The alternative corporate figure, Executive B, is a person for whom moral compass is not merely some expedient concern but rather a deeply held conviction fully evidenced in every aspect of life—including professional conduct. Nothing in this individual's work history would suggest any inclination toward some slick pragmatism, a fact fully recognized throughout the organization. Indeed, this executive enjoys a stellar reputation for integrity, transparency, and candor. All those who have worked with this executive clearly understand that this is an individual who can be counted upon to consistently operate in loyalty to principle, a person whose word can be taken as an ironclad guarantee. Not surprisingly, this manager has accumulated a fund of goodwill and trust throughout the institution. Superiors as well as subordinates are not only willing but eager for the opportunity to partner and collaborate with Executive B.

Increasingly, senior leadership has come to respect and value this executive as someone who not only gets the job done but also is capable of eliciting genuine commitment and loyalty from staff members—all of which contribute to a growing corporate consensus that this person is a rising star with a very bright future.

The Low Career Ladder	The High Career Ladder
Begins with blind and unlimited ambition	Begins with a strong conviction for professional conduct
Advances without respect for loyalty and principle	Advances with respect for loyalty and principle

Far too many corporate executives tend to believe that loyalty to principle is an obstacle to performance. Publicly, they may pay lip service to the virtues of "taking the high road," but in terms of personal conviction, these managers cynically dismiss ethical concerns as impediments to success. We believe that these views are not merely shortsighted; we see them as positively lethal to institutional attainment. In the larger economy of corporate life, negative traits such as fear, suspicion, deceitfulness, and so on are malignancies that inevitably fail to advance the interests of either the organization or the individual manager. When treachery and cunning become embedded features of a corporate culture, the institution is certain to forfeit the motivation and loyalty of its people. In the short term some of these duplicitous approaches may appear to pay dividends, but in the end they invariably result in extreme misfortune for the organization as well as for conniving administrators. And for those who find these claims extravagant, we respectfully offer the following roster of executives who felt the same way: Kenneth Lay, Dennis Kozlowski, and Bernie Madoff, among others.

When treachery and cunning take over an organization's culture:

- The institution forfeits the motivation and loyalty of its members.

- Trust in leadership is undermined.

- Misfortune results for both the conniving administrator and the organization.

In sum, it is essential that no leader slight or discount the wisdom conveyed in Sophoclean tragedy; to wit, that honesty, truthfulness, and integrity are invaluable aspects of human credibility. Minus such credibility, no manager can ever hope to attain the status of a real leader. When all is said and done, of the many things a person might hold dear in life, nothing is more dear (or more productive) than a good name. Accordingly, we encourage the modern leader to steer the course of Neoptolemus as opposed to the oily path of moral compromise advanced by Odysseus.

THE GOLDEN LEADERSHIP GRID

- Lead with honor, candor, and integrity, not with mischief, deceit, and wily words.

- Moral compass shouldn't be a convenience but rather a deeply held belief that guides every aspect of your personal and professional life.

- Following the moral path can bring pain in the short run, as cheating and deceit usually seem at first to beat honor and integrity. But that path can bring gains in the long term, as honor and integrity ultimately defeat cheating and deceit.

- Rather "fail with honor than win by cheating."

RULE 10

"Character is destiny."
—HERACLITUS

"Character" is the essence of the philosophy of leadership. The set of values leaders espouse, the priorities they embrace, and the life code they live by shape the future of the organizations they lead.

"Character is destiny"; true leadership begins within, not without.

Born to a distinguished family in the city-state of Ephesus, Heraclitus (535 BC–475 BC) is one of the most interesting pre-Socratic philosophers. In antiquity he was noted for both his cryptic sayings, which seemed every bit as ambiguous as anything uttered by the Oracle of Delphi, and for a variety of caustic assessments leveled at those traditionally seen as learned and wise.

Examples of the former include "The way up and down is one and the same" and "The thunder-bolt steers the universe," and of the latter his advice that great poets such as Homer and Archilochus be beaten and expelled from the poetic contests. Observations such as these earned Heraclitus two famous epithets in antiquity. One was the Greek term *ho Skoteinos*, meaning "the dark," a reference to the dense obscurities associated with his many maxims. The other refers to a reputed melancholia from which Heraclitus is said to have suffered as a result of humanity's incurable attachment to ludicrous and absurd thinking. This alleged depression earned him the title "the weeping philosopher."

Although Heraclitus apparently concerned himself with a wide variety of philosophical questions, there is one area in particular for which he is arguably most famous—the doctrine of the unity of opposites. From the very beginning of their rational inquiries, the ancient Greeks apparently believed that beneath the apparent jumble of physical objects and random motions there was a "cosmos" or unifying order. This assumption was driven by a vigorous refusal to view the world as little more than a kaleidoscope of discordant phenomena. Motivated by this conviction, the Greeks began their quest to discover the rational foundation of existence. For Thales, this underlying reality was water; for another thinker, named Anaximenes, air was the cohesive substance that lent unity and order to the world. Heraclitus took a different approach.

Rather than identify a natural element (water, air, etc.) as the unity bestowing the substratum of the world, his understanding of cosmos focused more on process. Specifically, Heraclitus argued that the turmoil and chaos we perceive in the world is chiefly the product of human misconception. Heraclitus did not deny the highly dynamic nature of the universe—indeed, according to Plato he advanced a theory of constant change, *panta rhei* ("all is flux"). But while it may be true, as Heraclitus said, that "nature loves to hide," her many transformative gestures are neither as disjointed nor as unmethodical as they may seem. In truth, the apparent disorder is part of a well-calibrated harmony in which change in one part of the system is matched by corresponding alterations in another area. There is, in short, a kind of cosmic economy operating in the universe that binds and unifies existence into a coordinated, comprehensive whole.

Significantly, there are no loose ends here. Nothing is excluded from this complex, orderly web of inter-relationships. And it was humanity's ongoing incapacity to grasp this abiding order that elicited Heraclitus's notorious indictments of the so-called "wise."

The scheme presented by Heraclitus is not simply a meditation on the mechanical operations of nature. We, too, are subject to this same system of actions and reactions, and it is in this context that Heraclitus offered the aphorism that serves as the focal point of our final chapter. The original source of this quote was undoubtedly Heraclitus's book *On Nature*, which addressed a broad range of issues including scientific, political, and metaphysical subjects. Unfortunately this book has been lost, but at least two later authors (Plutarch and John Stobaeus) certify the authenticity of the saying "A man's character is his destiny."

The concept of "destiny" has a variety of powerfully suggestive implications, all of which tend to relate to how one understands the role and significance of human will. There are many who see fate or destiny as an inexorable force in human affairs. According to this view, our decisions and actions are little more than impotent gestures that have no material effect upon the extent or quality of our lives; human will, no matter how well informed or disciplined, cannot alter the inexorable edicts of destiny. Not surprisingly, those who subscribe to this position often adopt passive if not fatalistic attitudes toward life. Ideas of human agency are replaced with images of men and women as the plaything of preordained powers that can be neither comprehended nor controlled. In a manner of speaking we are reduced to mere passengers in the journey of life. Every human being is preassigned a seat as well as a destination, but the why and the wherefore remain lamentably beyond our understanding.

Two Views About Destiny

Passive	Active
Our actions have no effect on our destiny	Our actions can shape our destiny
We cannot comprehend our fate	Destiny is character

To say the least, these perspectives offer a rather somber assessment of the human condition. They are, nevertheless, more common than one might think. Ask yourself, for instance, how often you have heard colleagues, friends, and family say something along the following lines: "What will be, will be"; "It was inevitable that something like this would happen"; "No one is to blame; it was fate." How are we to understand these sentiments and, more specifically, how are they to be understood in light of Heraclitus's aphorism?

Observations such as these are more than a bit disconcerting to the extent that they suggest the futility of human endeavor. If, indeed, we are little more than pawns in some grand, cosmic chess game whose logic and outcome are impossible to grasp, then what good are our plans, our efforts, our exertions? Why not simply submit to the enigmatic forces that remorselessly govern our lives?

It is precisely this sort of submissive thinking that Heraclitus intends to refute. The idea that "character is destiny" suggests that to some significant extent we are the architects of our own fate, that human will, intent, and decision genuinely matter. This is not to suggest that every activity or objective in life is guaranteed to comply with human aspiration. There are certainly many circumstances in life that lie beyond our control—including some that entail grave misfortune—and it is specifically those episodes that foster the impression that an ill-omened fate is perpetually ready to conspire against us. But even here, if we carefully examine the details underlying such ominous occasions, we often discover that ill-considered human activity, not a malignant fate, stands behind the lamentable occurrence. Take, for example, the skier who is swept away by an avalanche, or the golfer who dies by being struck by lightning.

What are the odds of something like this occurring? Are these not classic illustrations of how a malicious fate can brutally impose its verdicts upon the innocent? What we fail to consider in situations such as these is the fact that the skier ignored warnings of a high avalanche risk on the day of his demise and that the golfer insisted on completing his round of golf despite the obvious appearance of storm clouds. More often than not, what at first glance appears to be a completely arbitrary and capricious demonstration of destiny's heavy hand turns out to be a disaster of our own making. The skier and golfer perish not because their names were written in the "Book of Destiny"; their time was up because they exercised reckless options that greatly increased the probability of serious injury or death.

Be it hoped the implications of Heraclitus's epigram are becoming more clear. In the majority of cases, we are not marionettes dancing to the tune of some merciless fate. While we may be strongly inclined to identify destiny as the source of our disappointments and failures, in truth much of the responsibility is invariably our own. This is an important part of the message contained in the claim that "character is destiny." Who a person is—the values one espouses, the priorities one embraces, the life code by which one lives—inevitably plays a significant role in determining the quality and substance of an individual's life. For good or ill, character tends to be the prime determinant influencing virtually every facet of human experience—everything from our personal relationships to our professional lives.

Character Is Destiny

- Personal values, priorities, and life code determine the quality and substance of life.

- Personal and professional relations reflect the character of those involved.

We need to be clear about how the term "character" is being used in this context. Without qualification, the word should be understood as denoting a person's moral essence. Those of "good" character are individuals who acknowledge and respect the rights of others, who have the courage to accept responsibility for their own shortcomings, and who operate in loyalty to a personal code of conduct that lends meaning and integrity to their lives. In other words, men and women of good character have invested the necessary time and energy to assess and develop their potentials as authentic human beings. We believe these efforts are the building blocks of destiny in the sense that people of good character come to enjoy a unique wisdom stemming from a deep self-understanding; that is, from knowing themselves. It is above all this wisdom that helps shape the destiny of those we have defined as real leaders. We also believe that those deficient in this character-based wisdom will never realize their full range of potentials as either managers or as people. Here, we specifically refer to administrative personnel who routinely seek moral compromise as their first option and who define leadership as little more than an opportunity to exercise despotic authority. Mentalities such as these are also the stuff of destiny—destinies littered with wasted opportunities and unfulfilled potentials.

What shapes the character of a real leader?

- Acknowledgement and respect for the rights of others

- Courage to accept responsibility for one's own shortcomings

- Deep self-understanding—"knowing thyself"

In conclusion, we believe that Heraclitus was correct to insist that we are, to a very great extent, the authors of both our own blessings and our own burdens. Admittedly, there are occasional situations in which people find themselves victims of circumstances completely beyond their control. But these untoward episodes are far less common than we are typically inclined to believe. In the final analysis, the fault and the responsibility more often lies with us, not with the stars—Shakespeare and Heraclitus were in agreement on this point. The utility of this insight will not be lost on real leaders. Such men and women understand that their substance (character) as people will directly influence their "fate" as managers. Additionally, they will recognize that a well-formed character is the priceless reward paid to those who have done the hard work of coming to know themselves.

THE GOLDEN LEADERSHIP GRID

- The "fate" of organizations is not based on the stars. The character of an organization's leadership determines a company's destiny.

- The character of a real leader is the result of a carefully crafted philosophy of life.

- A leader's philosophy is constantly informed by moral considerations.

EPILOGUE

True leadership is not simply a matter of academic credential. What distinguishes the real leader, the man or woman who makes a tangible difference in the workplace, from a mere administrator is a unique series of perspectives and values. Where others become entangled in details and trivialities, genuine leaders employ methods and approaches reflecting a clarity and insight that come only from a well-examined life. Using principles such as those offered here, they skillfully weave an integrated and philosophically informed fabric that enriches and dignifies their lives. It is for this reason that real leaders are invariably an indispensable part of any organization's formula for success.

The authors are hopeful that the preceding pages have demonstrated one thing above all else: There is no "royal road" to leadership. On the contrary, achieving the rank of genuine leader is a daunting task that most will find prohibitively challenging. Among other things it involves an intimidating process of self-assessment in which light is cast upon those hidden truths we all tend to zealously conceal. Additionally, it requires a kind of moral stamina whereby ethically informed standards become regulative features of a person's life. In sum, leadership requires a special form of courage: the courage to "know thyself" and the courage to fashion a code of conduct governed by principled conviction.

1. **Know thyself.** Understand your inner world, your bright and dark sides, your personal strengths and weakness. Self-comprehension is a fundamental precondition necessary for real leadership.

2. **Office shows the person.** The assumption of authority brings out the leader's inner world. It reveals whether the leader has undergone a process of honest self-discovery that allows for the productive application of power.

3. **Nurture community in the workplace.** Community development and positive sentiment are virtues leaders must nurture by providing the right support, guidance, and incentives.

4. **Do not waste energy on things you cannot change.** Do not waste resources and energies on things you cannot control, and therefore, cannot change.

5. **Always embrace the truth.** Effective leaders should always embrace the truth, always encourage candid criticism throughout the organization, be skeptical of flattering appraisals, and never let authority place a wedge between them and the truth.

6. **Let competition reveal talent.** Nurture an environment that can use the forces of competition constructively, create a platform that releases the ingenuity and creativity of your employees in pursuing corporate goals and objectives, identify subordinates who use competition as a constructive force, steer away from subordinates who use competition as a destructive force.

7. **Live life by a higher code.** Dedicate yourself to a higher standard of personal conduct; don't harbor ill-will toward those who offend; be ready to assist those who are in need without asking something in return; remain calm in the face of crisis; dedicate yourself to principle without compromise; earn the trust, respect, and admiration of your subordinates through your character, not the authority conferred upon you by the corporate chart; turn authority into power.

8. **Always evaluate information with a critical eye.** Don't rely upon old premises, assertions, and theories. Develop a critical mindset that accepts nothing at face value, certify the credibility and usefulness of critical information, analyze the context that produces critical information and the messengers who convey it, and never rush to judgments.

9. **Never underestimate the power of personal integrity.** Personal integrity is a critical asset for real leadership. Always set an honorable agenda, adhere to a code of professional conduct, never try to justify dishonesty and deceit, rather "fail with honor than win by cheating."

10. **Character is destiny.** True leadership is ultimately traceable to factors of character and personal integrity; much of what is called "destiny" lies in our hands, not in mysterious forces beyond our control.

One final note: The authors recognize that for some readers what has been presented here will appear naively idealistic, that what we propose seems to tear at the fabric of common sense. We wish to assure those so inclined that we are not in the habit of tilting at windmills. We fully comprehend the hard realities and dark truths of administrative life—the politics, the intrigues, the treacheries. Accordingly, we do not endorse milquetoast models of management any more than we believe a few soothing words can result in all things becoming "sweetness and light." But at the same time, we are confident that the attainment of corporate objectives involves a good deal more than some cynical understanding of the term "expediency." We are convinced that enduring success is ultimately traceable to those rare men and women who, by virtue of their personal insights and integrity, are able to command the loyalties and commitments of their subordinates. To our way of thinking, failure to see matters in these terms constitutes the real naïveté as well as the greatest impediment to building a meaningful enterprise.

ABOUT THE AUTHORS

Michael A. Soupios is professor of political philosophy at LIU Post in New York, where he has taught and held a variety of administrative positions since 1977. The author of numerous articles and papers, Soupios has also written five books, including *The Ten Golden Rules* (with Panos Mourdoukoutas). In addition, he holds eight graduate degrees including four earned doctorates. His areas of expertise include history, classics, philosophy, political science, and religion. He has conducted seminars and special lectures in all these fields. Soupios resides in East Northport, New York, with his wife, Linda.

Panos Mourdoukoutas is professor and chair of the Department of Economics at LIU Post in New York. He has published several articles in professional journals and magazines, including Forbes.com (where he has his own column), *Barron's*, the *New York Times*, *Japan Times*, *Newsday*, *Plain Dealer*, *Edge Singapore*, *European Management Review*, *Management International Review*, and *Journal of Risk and Insurance*. He has also published twelve books, including *The Ten Golden Rules* (with Michael Soupios). He has traveled extensively throughout the world giving lectures and seminars for private and government organizations. His interests lie in global markets, business, investment strategy, and personal success.